WALKING WITH

Gosse

NATURAL HISTORY, CREATION AND RELIGIOUS CONFLICTS

To Kathryn,
with best wishes,
Roger -

ROGER S. WOTTON

First published in 2012 by Clio Publishing, Southampton, England.

http://www.cliopublishing.org

A full CIP record for this book is available from the British Library.

ISBN: 978-0-9556983-9-2

Designed and typeset by CARBON DESiGN Company // www.carbon.uk.com
Printed by Hobbs the Printer Ltd, Southampton, England.
http://www.hobbscolour.co.uk

Clio Publishing is committed to a sustainable future for our business, readers and the planet. The book in your hands is made from paper certified by the Forest Stewardship Council.

For Karen, Alexander and Anna.

About the author

Roger Wotton is an Emeritus Professor of Biology at University College London (UCL). He was born in Paignton, Devon, during the Great Blizzard of January 1947 and grew up in the town before leaving to study Zoology at Reading University. Roger then developed his interest in research in Freshwater Biology and was awarded an MSc at the University of Salford and a PhD at the University of Durham. He was appointed to a Demonstratorship in Zoology at the University of Newcastle-upon-Tyne in 1973 and this was followed by a Lectureship, then Senior Lectureship, in Biology at Goldsmiths' College London. In 1989, Roger was invited to join the Department of Zoology at University College London where he spent the rest of his academic career, having been made Professor of Biology in 2002.

Roger's research has focussed on the biology of organic matter in streams and rivers and he has worked in the United Kingdom, Sweden, Finland and the USA. He has published many research papers, the web book *Life in Water*, and he devised and edited both editions of the book *The Biology of Particles in Aquatic Systems*. A main focus of Roger's work has been to integrate ideas from all branches of aquatic science, from streams to oceans, resulting also in a number of wide-ranging reviews. These contributions to research and scholarship were acknowledged by the award of a DSc degree by Reading University. In addition to research, he has always enjoyed teaching and organising courses in general Zoology and in Aquatic Biology. His success as a teacher has been recognised by two Faculty Teaching Awards and a Provost's Teaching Award. In addition to academic studies and teaching, Roger also enjoys writing and lecturing on general topics, especially those relating to Biology and mythology.

Roger is married to Karen, a teacher, and they have two grown-up children, Alexander and Anna. He lives in Berkhamsted and among his interests are Natural History, wine, fine dining, horse racing, elephant watching, and railways.

Contents

Henry and Edmund

Back to the Present

Acknowledgements

Dr Susan England of Clio Publishing deserves special thanks for seeing my initial, clumsy manuscript through to publication. I have valued her many helpful suggestions and constant support throughout the past few months. Thanks also to John Somers for designing the book and cover and to Dr Bob Carling who put me in contact with Clio Publishing.

Sources of material used in the preparation of the book are acknowledged in footnotes to the text and under each illustration, and I would like to thank the Zoological Society of London (ZSL) and Torquay Museum Society for allowing me to read the First Editions by Philip Henry Gosse that are held in their libraries. Dr Ann Thwaite, the author of the definitive biographies of both Philip Henry and Edmund Gosse, was kind in replying very quickly to my letters and I was very pleased that Professor Sir Patrick Bateson FRS, the President of the ZSL, agreed to write the Foreword. Thanks also to Dorothy Jefferson for allowing me to visit Sandhurst in St Marychurch, the Gosse family home for many years.

I have received encouragement from many people during the two years I was working on the book. Special thanks go to my brothers, David and Geoffrey, and to Patrick and Tarja Armitage who have always been positive in their support.

Finally, I could not have written the book without the tolerance and love of my wife Karen, especially during 'Henry Days', when I seemed to be lost somewhere in the nineteenth century.

Foreword

In April 2010, the Zoological Society of London commemorated the bicentenary of the birth of Philip Henry Gosse with an article on their website. Henry Gosse was well-known as a writer and illustrator of books on Natural History and he encouraged his readers to collect animals and plants and to observe them in their natural surroundings. It was Gosse who popularised the design and maintenance of aquarium tanks and he supplied material for the Aquarium at the London Zoo. The website article contains the following quotation, describing his involvement:

> Early in December, 1852, I put myself into communication with the Secretary of the Zoological Society, and the result was the transfer of a small collection of the Zoophytes and Annelides, which I had brought up from Ilfracombe and which I had kept for two months in cases in London, – to one of the tanks in the new Fish House just erected in the Society's Gardens in Regent's Park. This little collection thus became the nucleus and the commencement of the Marine Aquarium afterwards exhibited there.

Henry Gosse is most widely known as being the father in *Father and Son*, which was published anonymously by his son Edmund in 1907, nearly twenty years after Henry's death. This shows us another side of Henry's life, for he was a member of the Brethren and a believer in the literal truth of the Bible, including the contradictory accounts of the Creation given in Genesis. Edmund found him oppressive, and he was certainly unyielding in his religious beliefs. Even so, he struggled to reconcile his belief in the literal truth of the Bible with the geological concepts of time that were gaining acceptance in the mid-Nineteenth cntury. Henry Gosse wrote *Omphalos* to 'untie the geological knot.' He argued that all living things were created just a few thousand years ago, but the rock strata showed evidence of an earlier existence. Such a theory satisfied neither the creationists nor the evolutionists when the book was published in 1857, but adverse responses surprised and hurt Gosse.

He recovered from this blow, and from the larger one of the loss of his first wife Emily to breast cancer. He remained for the rest of his life in Torquay in Devon, moving there with Edmund just before *Omphalos* was published. Father and son spent much time together collecting and sorting organisms from the shore and Henry recovered all his old enthusiasm for Natural History. It was a happy time for both of them, and made all the happier when Henry married his second wife Eliza and when Edmund, as a boy of ten, became an adult member of the local Brethren congregation that Henry led. The close bond between father and son then slowly weakened as the adolescent Edmund could no longer share Henry's beliefs. The rift between them widened when Edmund moved to London and began his career as a librarian, scholar and civil servant. Edmund mixed with the intellectual élite of the time and was recognised with a knighthood and the Légion d'Honneur. *Father and Son* was recognised then as a masterpiece and it continues to have that status today. It is a moving book that tells just how damaging religion can be, while recognising that Henry Gosse was a major figure in the developing interest of Victorians in Natural History. His books – even *Omphalos* – deserve to be more widely known than they are today.

His immovable religious stance has relevance today when creationist beliefs are growing in strength. How could an obviously intelligent man with a deep knowledge of Natural History have not wondered where the sons of Adam and Eve might have obtained their wives? Puzzling, indeed. Above all, though, Henry's infectious enthusiasm for Biology, which comes through so well in this book, is how he should be remembered.

Professor Sir Patrick Bateson FRS
President of the Zoological Society of London.

Philip Henry Gosse, by Devonian photographer, William Widger, c. 1862. (Attribution unknown). [From Thwaite, *Glimpses of the Wonderful*]

Preface

My interest in Philip Henry Gosse was kindled by the excellent biography, *Glimpses of the Wonderful, The Life of Philip Henry Gosse* [1] by Dr Ann Thwaite. I had heard of him; knew of his reputation as a Natural Historian, and was aware that the rocky shores in Torbay where Henry Gosse collected were among those I so enjoyed investigating as a child. *Glimpses of the Wonderful* introduced me to the man behind the Natural History; his profound belief in the literal truth of The Bible, and the complex and difficult relationship he had with his son, Edmund.

Edmund was a member of the literary Establishment at the beginning of the last century and was knighted for services to the Arts. His autobiographical memoir *Father and Son, A Study of Two Temperaments* [2] is his best-known book and it describes Edmund's childhood, the difficulties of coping with the illness and death of his mother while still a child, and his struggle to break away from his father's controlling religious views. Henry's image has never recovered from the portrayal in Edmund's book, but Henry also did himself no favours by publishing a book, *Omphalos* [3] in which he developed a nonsensical theory of 'prochronic' existence to show that the description of Creation in Genesis did not conflict with the idea of geological time. While the theory was revelatory to Henry, it was poorly received by almost everyone else, and *Omphalos* was dismissed by the scientific community and religious believers alike. Henry was surprised and upset by this reaction, although he would not have been if he had stood back and thought about the potential reception of his revelation.

So, this is the negative view of Henry Gosse, but anyone reading early editions of his Natural History books will see a quite different side of the man. He wrote wonderfully and had the gift, and training, of an artist, so his books had illustrations of rare quality, and perusing First Editions gives an indication of how stunning they appeared to their Victorian audience. A full, annotated bibliography of Henry Gosse's publications has been made by Richard Freeman and Douglas Wertheimer and their detailed volume, *Philip Henry Gosse: A Bibliography*, [4] was an invaluable source of information in the preparation of *Walking with Gosse*, as was Edmund's earlier biography of his father, *The Naturalist of the Sea-Shore; The Life of Philip Henry Gosse*. [5] Henry's first books were about his travels in Canada and in the West Indies, interspersed with volumes on religious themes, or educational books on Biology for the Society for Promoting Christian Knowledge, with books of this type continuing to appear throughout his productive years. It was with *A Naturalist's Rambles on the Devonshire Coast* [6] and *The Aquarium: an unveiling of the wonders of the deep sea* [7] that Henry became widely known, and his fame resulted in lecture tours and popular acclaim. After *Omphalos*, there were also two interesting volumes on *The Romance of Natural History* [8] where Henry showed his 'poetic' side, expanding into a wider view of Nature. Henry Gosse also wrote scientific works and his contribution was recognised when he was made a Fellow of the Royal Society.

Walking with Gosse begins with autobiography, as I have had a love of Nature for as long as I can remember, and our family were Christians, although we attended a Baptist Church, rather different to the Brethren congregation that Henry Gosse led. I can thus empathise with aspects of Henry and aspects of Edmund and a further similarity to their story is that my mother also became ill and died when I was young. Having a feeling for both father and son makes their conflict only too real to me and, while I so much admire Henry Gosse the Natural Historian and communicator, I cannot accept his religious position, or his views on Creation. It might be thought that the story of Henry and Edmund Gosse is locked in the Victorian and Edwardian eras, but it has a resonance with debates that are taking place today: on evolution and creation; on the importance of Nature, and on the need for religious tolerance. The book thus closes with a discussion of these contemporary issues.

A note on the use of Philip Henry Gosse's first names

My use of Henry as Gosse's preferred name follows the lead taken by Ann Thwaite in *Glimpses of the Wonderful*. In the Introduction to the 2007 edition of her biography of Edmund, *Edmund Gosse: A Literary Landscape*, [9] she states that Henry 'was the name by which he was usually known', and Emily, his first wife, certainly called him Henry (from sources quoted by Edmund in *Father and Son*). However, Eliza, his second wife, refers to P. H. Gosse as Philip in Appendix 1 of *The Naturalist of the Sea-Shore* and Edmund also used Philip here, perhaps in deference to his step-mother's wishes. Letters seem to have been signed P. H. Gosse and books, Philip Henry Gosse.

1 Thwaite, A, *Glimpses of the Wonderful: The Life of Philip Henry Gosse*, (Faber and Faber), London, 2002.

2 Gosse, E, *Father and Son. A Study of Two Temperaments*, (William Heinemann), London, 1907.

3 Gosse, P. H., *Omphalos: an attempt to untie the geological knot*, (John Van Voorst), London.

4 Freeman, R. B., and Wertheimer, D, *Philip Henry Gosse: A Bibliography*, (Dawson Publishing), Folkestone, 1980.

5 Gosse, E, *The Naturalist of the Sea-Shore; The Life of Philip Henry Gosse*, (K. Paul, Trench, Trübner & Co., Ltd), London, 1890.

6 Gosse, P. H., *A Naturalist's Rambles on the Devonshire Coast*, (John Van Voorst), London, 1853.

7 Gosse, P. H., *The Aquarium: an unveiling of the wonders of the deep sea*, (John Van Voorst), London, 1854.

8 Gosse, P. H., *The Romance of Natural History [First and Second Series]*, (J. Nisbet and Co.), London, 1860 and 1861.

9 Thwaite, A, *Edmund Gosse: A Literary Landscape, 1849-1925,* (The History Press), Stroud, 2007.

How I Encountered
Henry Gosse

Growing up at the seaside

Oh! I do like to be beside the seaside
I do like to be beside the sea!
I do like to stroll upon the Prom, Prom, Prom!
Where the brass bands play:
"Tiddely-om-pom-pom!"
So just let me be beside the seaside
I'll be beside myself with glee
And there's lots of girls beside,
I should like to be beside
Beside the seaside!
Beside the sea!

Chorus of a Music Hall song written by John A. Glover-Kind, 1907.

After the holiday season, Paignton in the 1950s was typical of many seaside towns in the UK, being quiet and left to its residents. A small theatre put on a rather good amateur pantomime and, at other times, hosted school music festivals and the occasional Billy Graham-style revivalist meeting.

The local community was supported by a number of churches, grocery shops, newsagents, outfitters, and the usual array of shops to be found on high streets at that time and there were dentists, General Practitioners and a small hospital. My family had lived in Paignton for years and we didn't travel much beyond the town and the surrounding area, with Bristol seeming like the far north. We made occasional trips to Plymouth to see Auntie Annie but the places we read about in the *News Chronicle*, or heard mentioned on the BBC Home Service, seemed very remote indeed.

It was during the summer that Paignton came alive and we locals then shared the town with thousands of holidaymakers, usually families enjoying their summer break and groups of young people looking to meet others. The holiday season began rather quietly, with Guest Houses opening to welcome older, more sedate visitors in May and June, and built up to a peak in August. Trainloads of holidaymakers came from all parts of the country, but especially from the Midlands. Saturday was changeover day in the holiday accommodation and the platforms of Paignton Railway Station were nearly always crowded on Saturdays, with one set of passengers being replaced by another in both directions. For me this was exciting. Not watching the crowds of visitors, who were just a blur, but the chances for train spotting and seeing railway engines from, to me, distant places far beyond Bristol. I don't know why train spotting was such a passion, but it was. It became like a religion. Even today, the smell of privet flowers reminds me of happy walks through the local park to the Railway Station. It was a smell that brought the expectancy of a good day's worship.

Summer trains became less busy in the late 1960s and more visitors arrived in Paignton by coach (we called coaches charabancs, pronounced sharra*bangs*); then private cars became the most popular form of transport and part of Victoria Park was turned into a car and coach park to accommodate the influx. The town was never as busy as in the 1950s and early 1960s, but there were so many cars that the original site quickly required the building of a multi-storey car park. This very ugly building remains today.

Holidaymakers probably had little interest in the trains in which they travelled, although they would have noticed that many of the carriages were old, as they were only used on summer Saturdays. The trains invariably ran late and parents had the challenge of keeping young children occupied. Still, there was the seaside to look forward to on the way down and happy memories on the way back. Most visitors to the town stayed in Guest Houses and small Hotels, although there were some holiday chalets and caravan parks that were looked down upon by the more established Paigntonians. Many of the Hotels were in the rows of stately villas built in Victorian times for wealthy residents and for those who could afford to make frequent visits to be near the sea for its beneficial effects, and even to bathe. As in the 1950s, Victorian visitors travelled to the coast by train and Torquay, with its Italianate influence, was the more prestigious part of the 'English Riviera'. Little of this history was known to me as a boy and the atmosphere in Paignton during the nineteenth century would have been quite different to the one with which I was familiar.

The most popular activities for 1950s visitors were sitting on the beach, playing in the sand, taking a swim, or maybe enjoying a boat trip around the bay, or a train ride down to Kingswear and on by ferry to Dartmouth. Then, as now, a dominant feature of Dartmouth was the Britannia Royal Naval College, where the Queen met Prince Philip (and how often has that phrase been repeated down the years?). The marvellous old buildings and distinguished history of the town were somehow of lesser significance. There were also coach trips to Dartmoor and to country villages and, in the evening, excursions ran to various old inns. However, most holidaymakers stayed in the town.

I know nothing of the catering at breakfast or dinner in the Guest Houses and Hotels, but much candyfloss, sticky sweets and Paignton Rock were consumed throughout the day and it wasn't possible to walk far without the aroma of deep-fat fryers cooking either chips or doughnuts. The shops and sales cabins near the sea front were solely for the holidaymakers and those outlets that didn't sell food, sold 'Kiss Me Quick' hats, saucy postcards and other ephemera, with sales of plastic-smelling Pacamacs being good in some years. While some of my friends joined in with the visitors, our family did not. It wasn't because we thought we were better than them; we just didn't go to the beach as a family. I went with friends for an occasional dip, but was always so scared of the water that I never managed to get beyond paddling and jumping up and down through incoming waves. I preferred places along the coast that were more secluded and, to me, more interesting. Some visitors also ventured to coves, pools and quiet beaches with good strand lines, but most preferred to be part of the happy throng.

In late September, the activity of summer had disappeared. Seafront shops and cabins were still in place, but they were boarded up as there were no customers, and storms could be damaging during autumn and winter. The nearer one moved to the sea, the more shops were closed in winter. The main shopping street in Paignton was bisected by the railway line and the section that ran from the level crossing to the sea front was called Torbay Road. In addition to the gift shops, ice cream parlours, cafés and slot machine arcades, some shops along Torbay Road were open throughout the year. Among these were 'May's Bakery' (where I bought pasties, to provide energy for train spotting), 'Outsize Gowns' (for ladies with a fuller figure), and the two 'Perrett's of Paignton' outfitters; the men's shop and the ladies' shop being separated by 20 metres or so. The Perrett's men's shop was where my father worked for many years, spending some of that time as manager. It was a traditional outfitters, with suits from famous names of the time such as DAKS and Chester Barrie, and my father enjoyed working there, meeting regular customers, providing a good service, and using conversations to keep informed about local activities. Local goings-on were one of his major interests, together with Freemasonry. Mr Perrett Senior had retired from the business by the time I remember it, to be replaced by his sons Mr John and Mr Peter. Just seeing their names written in that way reminds me of how traditional the shop was. Dad had a favourite phrase – 'Manners Maketh Man' – and his courtesy was appreciated by customers and colleagues alike: he was never obsequious but, typically, 'knew his place.' His salesmanship and knowledge of outfitting were certainly important to the firm and he accompanied Mr John on annual trips to London to see the latest fashions and, I presume, to meet with suppliers.

Being a Christian

We were members of Winner Street Baptist Church in Paignton. It was not a 'fire and brimstone chapel', more a place for families to meet to hear The Word and to socialise. Rousing hymns were led by a choir, with adults in pews on one side and children (including me) in matching pews on the other side, both of which faced the congregation. Those of us in the choir were therefore able to get a good view of who had their eyes closed during prayers, who was looking around at the latest provincial fashions, and who was fidgeting or writing notes. Communion was taken from a table between the choir pews but this ceremony was always a mystery to me, as children were not permitted to attend until after baptism – adult baptism, of course.

At home, we didn't have family prayers, or prayers before meals, but did make an annual religious pilgrimage – well, a short walk – on Good Friday to a local wood, where egg sandwiches and crisps were the exciting outdoor lunch and both seemed to be reserved for this particular picnic. We sang 'There is a Green Hill Far Away without a City Wall' as we walked and I remember finding it odd that some green hills are surrounded by city walls. I put it down to another mystery of religion, as there was much that I failed to understand in those days. It's the same now.

Family group in July 1948. From left to right: Mum holding RSW (aged 1); Gramp; eldest brother David standing above elder brother Geoffrey; Nan; unknown; Dad. (From Author's Collection).

A country walk, August Bank Holiday 1950. From left to right: Mum, RSW (aged 3), David and Geoffrey. (From Author's Collection).

David, Geoffrey and RSW (aged 5) dressed up for the Winner Street Baptist Church Anniversary, 1952 (we rarely had legs in those days!) (From Author's Collection).

Services of baptism at Winner Street were rather strange and unsettling, although I only attended two. One was for my elder brother and I can't remember who was being baptised in the second, but it was likely to be a relative or close friend. I recollect the minister conducting the ceremony walking into the baptismal pool followed one at a time by each candidate, dressed in one of the long white gowns which had been made by Mrs Pike, a member of the congregation. For each candidate came the solemn, 'I baptise you (or was it thee?) in the name of... (I can't remember the rest)', followed by a backwards dip to be completely immersed. Each successful entrant into full membership of the church was then lifted up and made a soggy walk to the back vestry accompanied by a supporter and the sound of joyous hymn singing. Then it was the turn of the next person and the procedure was repeated until all had been baptised. With my fear of water I hated the thought of immersion, so didn't think that I would ever be baptised. I was too young to be a candidate anyway, but if the idea of sending me to the services was to encourage me to think about a future possibility, it had the opposite effect. It wasn't just the immersion; the whole atmosphere was filled with an unpleasant emotion. Or perhaps the emotion was fine but there was too much of it? I still feel uncomfortable with the emotionality of evangelical Christian movements, yet a heightened state that borders on mild hysteria seems to be so important to many believers.

During the school summer holidays, Paignton had visits from the CSSM (Children's Special Service Mission) and their meetings were held on the Green at the seafront. The enthusiastic young leaders set up a banner, gave us the message and led lots of singing, usually of hymns and songs I knew from Winner Street. The preaching passed me by as, like the hymns, there were familiar words, but they had little meaning for me. Yet, overall, the meetings were quite fun and had the atmosphere of a holiday camp, albeit an evangelical one. One year, the CSSM leaders also included an African and this was something very exotic for us at the time, as Paignton was one hundred percent white. I can't remember much about him other than that he taught us the hymn 'Yes, Jesus Loves Me' in his language. I don't know if my recall is accurate, but I think it went: 'A Jesu femi / A Jesu femi / A Jesu femi / Bibeli so fa me.' It was something like that and it impressed me. Here was a link to the mission fields and the missionaries who had such a high status in the church. So high, that there were even regular collections for them.

I left the congregation of Winner Street Baptist Church when I was 11 years old as I couldn't relate either to the people there, or to the message. Although probably believing that the Bible must be a true record, it didn't mean that much to me or, apparently, to many of those who attended the Church. Perhaps that is unfair. What I realised was that religious faith was never going to be simple for me and scepticism about many things, not just religion, was developing with the onset of adolescence. Although I had friends, I was a loner as far as thinking about things was concerned and I felt sure there was little chance that I would become 'born again' in the near future.

Dad agreed that I could leave Winner Street provided that I attended the local branch of the Crusaders Union. I cannot remember why we came to this agreement, but until I was 15 years old, Sunday afternoons were now spent with the Paignton Crusaders. We met in a rather bleak room in the local YMCA and were led first by Doc Sarson, who owned 'Sarson's the Chemists', and then by Mr Clifford who owned 'Outsize Gowns', the shop which was located just a few doors from 'Perrett's', where my father worked. Both leaders were members of the local Plymouth Brethren chapel. Doc Sarson was a kindly, white-haired man, from a very different generation to us young people and I can remember little else about Doc, but memories of Mr Clifford are imprinted more firmly. He was dynamic, arranged trips, and sometimes allowed us to ride in his 3.4 litre Mark II Jaguar. Now, that is a leader with appeal to adolescent boys. His daughter always played the piano for our singing of rousing religious songs like 'Onward Christian Soldiers' and 'He Who Would Valiant Be', and his son, David, a marine engineer, took us on trips when he was home from sea. On one occasion it was a cruise in a hired boat on the River Dart and we became grounded off Stoke Gabriel for a time, until the tide lifted us once again. Mr Clifford's kindness extended beyond Crusaders and he took time to ferry me to see my father when he was in hospital, waiting outside in his car while I did so. Once I left Crusaders I lost touch with him, but heard later that he underwent stomach surgery and, I think, left Paignton.

A last contact with formal Christianity came when I was at Torquay Boys' Grammar School and attending meetings of the Christian Union, in which my elder brother was a leader. We sat around a table and listened to speakers, or to tapes of Billy Graham preaching, and we also had prayer meetings when all present had to take part, each giving their little piece. Prayers were for the usual things connected with our salvation but, being at school, we also prayed for masters who were Christians, to boost their religious, as well as their educational, mission. I always dreaded prayer meetings and was not comfortable at any of the other meetings either. Unlike some of those present, I found Billy Graham strange and rather too energetic and neither could I summon up much enthusiasm for a guest speaker who spent many minutes propounding the correct pronunciation of Bethphage (it's Beth-fadjy not Beth-faije, if you see what I mean).

There were also tracts for us to hand out in the school, delivered in bulk from the Evangelical Tract Society. Have I remembered accurately that one of these was entitled, 'How I found God in Ramsgate Harbour', or is my mind playing tricks? Anyway, I couldn't hand out such things and had quite a collection by the time I stopped attending the Christian Union. Whether at home, at the Winner Street Baptist Church, at Crusaders, or at school there was little discussion of evolution and other interesting ideas. On leaving Christianity, I felt free and could think my own thoughts on creation and on any other issue. That was on the plus side. On the minus side were anxieties about death and Divine Judgement, which are familiar to many who leave behind a strong Christian upbringing. Those anxieties can continue for a long time.

Schools, parents, and my interest in Natural History

Shyness was always one of my problems. It was manageable when I was among friends or classmates at Oldway Primary School, but I had a fear of going into shops and having to ask for something. I don't know where the shyness came from (perhaps it was genetic?) but one result was that speaking in public was agony. I now realise that it's a common feeling and can be overcome with practice, but at that age I thought it just affected me. Anyway, Oldway Primary had an important anniversary to celebrate and, as I spoke well in class, myself and another pupil were asked to propose a vote of thanks to one of the main guests. After a lot of anxiety, I realised I couldn't go through with it and asked to be replaced before the ceremony. Anxiety played its part in my involvement with sports as well. The school competed in the regional Primary School sports day and I was part of a relay team where each member had to bounce a ball into a hoop on the ground, collect it, repeat this three more times and then return to the next team mate. We practised it many times in the school playground and I was as fast as any but, come the day of the event, I was so nervous that I didn't catch the ball from the first bounce but instead sent it off to one side. By the time I'd recovered, we had lost hopelessly and, although no-one said anything, not even 'Bad luck', I remember feeling very self conscious.

RSW, age 9, at Oldway Primary School. (From Author's Collection).

Most of my memories from Oldway are much better. Country Dancing was part of the school curriculum and I really enjoyed that, especially as I thought my partner was marvellous. She probably had no idea of this infatuation and, if she did, was not going to acknowledge it. However, it made 'Galopede' and other dances immensely enjoyable, if a little charged. Of course, my shyness was ever-present, but our partners were arranged for us by the teachers and they had treated me kindly. I'm not sure that everyone was as lucky. It's odd that I enjoyed country dancing so much, as I now strongly dislike having to dance and went through agonies approaching girls during dances in the 1960s and 1970s, often watching enviously from the sidelines and feeling paralysed. On occasions when courage didn't fail, I would be overcome with self-consciousness about my awkward movements and a feeling that I must look a fool. But all that was to come much later.

Lessons at Oldway Primary were enjoyable and I was lucky that most learning came easily to me. Although lazy by nature, I started to write a little book when I was seven and managed to keep going for a few chapters. It was about Jare the Pirate and was not, as would be expected, derivative as we weren't a literary family and I hadn't read any pirate stories, or even heard them on the wireless. The idea came from the mystery of sea caves around the coast in Torbay and my imagination of what adventures may have taken place in them over the years. The book petered out without a conclusion, but the hand-written pages were all stapled together and kept for a number of years in the family. I had to read some of it aloud to the rest of the class as it was being written.

All classrooms had a Nature Table and I was as drawn to this as I was to the coastline of Torbay. Each Table had twigs and leaves of various trees, the occasional disused bird's nest, egg shells or owl pellets. There were also living animals like earthworms moving through layers of coloured soil and mixing them. I don't think I was very questioning of what I saw, but it was fascinating, and I loved Nature Study, as it was called. In the final year at Primary School, Miss Bedford asked us to produce a pressed flower collection in our own time. My elder brother (three year's older than me) had already made one in his final year, so beating that was the first challenge. I soon became absorbed by the task and collected plants on my mostly solitary walks. On returning home, these were carefully laid out on the dining room table, identified with the help of books and then each was arranged between sheets of tissue paper which, in turn, were layered between heavy books. After pressing and drying, the plants were placed into a book with pages of blue paper and held using thin strips of sticky paper, with the common name of each plant being written alongside using white crayon. In a childlike way it was quite artistic (I knew nothing of blue Jasperware Wedgwood pottery at this time, but you can imagine how the collection looked). The plants were arranged at random and there were many more than my brother had managed to collect. I carried the book very carefully to school and was hopeful that I would win the First Prize, especially as there were so few 'serious' entries. However, it was not to be and I came second. The winner was my country dancing partner, whose father, Leslie Jackman, was a well-known local teacher, naturalist and broadcaster. Her collection was so much better than mine, so losing to Diane wasn't a body blow.

It was at about this time, that my two brothers and I were given a small microscope by Gramp, my maternal grandfather. Gramp was a retired baker and both stern and rigid in his views. We disliked each other intensely but he came to our house at least once a week and helped in any way that he could. I couldn't stand Gramp's little moralising talks, accompanied by the jingling of the coins he used to jiggle around in his pocket. The microscope was, however, a typically kind gift and this was the first time I'd been able to use one. Most terrestrial creatures that were easily collected moved around too rapidly for its narrow field of view, so we looked mainly at static objects. Favourites were salt and sugar crystals, or tomato ketchup with its flowing movements in red and oily yellow, which looked like the light shows that formed a background to 1960s pop culture. It didn't occur to me to use this small instrument to look at natural water samples and the tiny creatures they contain. Perhaps that reflects my lack of imagination, but it was really little more than a toy. Now, if it had been a low-power stereomicroscope with good illumination …

Other strong memories from Oldway Primary days are of the irregular school trips to interesting places like Torquay Pottery and to the local shore to look in rock pools, which certainly suited me. At low tide, we turned over stones in Fairy Cove next to Paignton Harbour to see crabs scuttling around. There were also so many other things to see: contracted and unpleasantly squidgy sea anemones; barnacles; mussels and limpets attached to the rocks; drying bladder wrack; 'mermaid's purses', and so much more. The advantage over the Nature Table was that almost all we saw was alive and *in situ* even though we could not see how everything looked when covered by the tide. However, that was possible with a visit to the Aquarium on the south side of Paignton Harbour, run by Leslie Jackman, the teacher and broadcaster who had guided my country dancing partner with her pressed flower collection. Although I visited the sea shore many times to look at rock pools, or turn over stranded weed on the beach to watch sandhoppers jump away, I didn't often go to the Aquarium as it brought on the same shyness I felt when going into shops. When I did visit, it was magical, even with its small tanks. There was such movement and colour, and above all a strong feeling of this being an alien world. Of course, my terror of putting my head under water would never allow me to watch the real thing so close by.

This interest in animals and plants wasn't confined to the coast. Our small, extended family took occasional bus rides into the countryside and we walked into woods to pick wild flowers; acceptable then, but rather frowned on now. I also took many walks on my own to pick flowers, or just for enjoyment. As no-one in our family had a car, and I never learned to ride a bicycle, walking in the Devon countryside was one of my great pleasures, alongside train spotting, and I often kept on for miles and miles. Although I had some good friends, with whom I played cricket or football, or with whom I played indoors with train sets, I was happy in my own company on these country walks. They started from home, or after a short bus journey, and I especially enjoyed being by streams and rivers, although accessing them by using tracks through woods would sometimes scare me a bit. I think I was afraid that there would be spooks or goblins or something rather than being afraid that I might encounter threatening strangers. Although I was sometimes frightened I might fall in, I was happy to pick up stones from the stream and river margins and observe rather different creatures to the familiar ones from the coast. There were crawling flatworms, leeches, and insect larvae of many kinds and habits. I didn't really know what they were and didn't find out more by looking at books. I should have done, as I loved reading encyclopaedias and found them absorbing.

I passed the 11 Plus examination and moved from Oldway Primary to Torquay Boys' Grammar School in autumn 1958, having taken the examination papers at Tweenaway Secondary Modern School, so we didn't have the comfort of 'playing at home'. A list of those who had passed was read out weeks later by Miss Bedford and I was pleased that my friends were also going to TBGS and less pleased that we would now be attending a boys' only school, the girls going to quite separate ones. This was something I remember especially strongly. At the end of the day I ran back home to tell my mother the good news and she was cooking at our ancient gas stove when I arrived, so the best way she could find of expressing her feelings was to pick up a tea towel and throw it at me. We didn't go in for hugging, or physical displays of affection in the family and this was my mother's way of showing delight. Of course, she also said how pleased she was. My mother seemed to find most aspects of life difficult, not just the emotional ones, and she was very thin and seemed to worry about everything all the time. She died within two years of this happy occasion when I was 13 and she 49. I think I gained my anxious streak from her, but don't know if this is genetic, or whether it was learned from her attitude to life.

Mum had been breaking blood vessels for some time and I remember looking into my parents' bedroom and seeing her in bed with fresh blood on the sheets. I think the blood had just been vomited and this incident followed a number of other mishaps, so she was taken to hospital to see if anything could be done to treat her condition. The family believed she would be coming home in a few weeks and there was a flurry of activity in anticipation. Dad bought a commode so that Mum wouldn't have to climb the stairs to go to the lavatory, and an occasional cleaner, Mrs Wynn, was taken on to help with the house. Miss Jones from Winner Street Baptist Church also came to cook for my father at lunch times. All these changes seemed odd, and worrying, to a sensitive soul like me and the commode somehow became a symbol of a loss of hope. Mum didn't come home. She was moved to a smaller hospital and then to another hospital five miles away in Totnes where she had a bed in a geriatric ward. She died in April 1960 and the cause of death on the certificate was cerebral haemorrhage resulting from malignant hypertension (medical language for a stroke caused by uncontrollable high blood pressure). True to form, I didn't go to the funeral at Winner Street Church, or the cremation in Torquay, but went instead for a walk in the country to grieve in my own way. I had only rarely seen Mum well and in good spirits, and my reaction to her death was typical of the young. I returned to a new style of day-to-day life quickly. There must have been emotional bruises and I was certainly not less shy and timid for the experience. However, the coast and countryside were constants and there was school work to get on with. There was still train-spotting too, although only for a year or so more before I lost interest.

Mum's illness and death had a devastating effect on my father. He was a diabetic and had suffered poor circulation and angina but I had no idea what these conditions meant at the time. I wanted to be close to him but somehow we both found it difficult to make emotional contact. Nonetheless, there was certainly a lot of emotion when Dad had a heart attack in the middle of the night (I cannot recall the year, but it was probably 1961). We didn't have a telephone and one of us boys had to rush out to a call box to ring for an ambulance. None of us knew what to do and Dad was clearly in pain and fear, calling out at one point, 'I'm coming Dor' as he thought he was dying and was about to go to Heaven to be re-united with my mother, Doris. Clearly, his Christian faith was intact, even during this very frightening experience. Dad came through this critical phase and was in hospital for weeks, while my brothers and I largely looked after ourselves. We had great support from the family, especially from Auntie Phyll and Uncle Wal (my Mum's sister and brother-in-law) and from Miss Jones. We muddled through and Dad was so impressed by our ability to cope that he gave each of us three boys a watch but, although discharged, he was clearly ill, with the diabetes unstable. To predict the correct dosage of insulin to be injected every morning, Dad had to make daily urine tests using a 'Clinitest' kit and, unfortunately he made up some of the results for whatever reason. This resulted in inadequate treatment from the Diabetes Clinic at Torbay Hospital, but what could they do if provided with inaccurate information? I think the whole situation was getting too much for him.

From 1962, when both my brothers had left home, the unstable diabetes came to dominate Dad's life and mine. As a young boy, I had always enjoyed looking out from my parents' bedroom window to watch for him coming home from work in the evening. I would pull the curtains vigorously from side-to-side to show Dad that I had seen him walking towards us along the road from Victoria Park. As this road faced our house, the sight of the curtains moving was meant as an advance welcome before I ran downstairs to greet him. Now I looked out to see whether he was walking erratically and, if he was, I made tea containing sugar to counteract the obvious insulin reaction. Normally, Dad could taste sugar readily but not on these occasions. It wasn't a constant threat, but there was always anxiety that he would have a reaction. Coming home from school as a 15 to 18 year-old was not fun and it may explain why I continued contact with the Christian Union, at least for a while. I also worried about how the insulin reactions were perceived at Perrett's, especially as the symptoms could resemble drunkenness and there was often a strong chemical smell on his breath. I never discovered how Mr John and Mr Peter reacted to his condition but they must have been concerned.

Dad died of a heart attack when I was 21 and I was told by a policeman who came to the door of the scruffy house in Manchester where I had a rented bed-sitting room. I had been half expecting this news but it was distressing when it happened, especially as he had died alone. After a miserable few days spent with friends, I then travelled to Paignton to clear out our old family home and pack up a case of valuable personal things which my eldest brother was to keep for me. I was only re-united with that case three years ago, as there was never an opportunity for me to collect it before. It contained some letters, a pair of pyjamas, a small trouser press and some bric-a-brac. What kind of mental state must I have been in when I packed that? Typically, I didn't attend Dad's funeral and cremation and went for a walk into the countryside instead, just as I had done after Mum's death. It seems that at 21, just as at 13, it was the natural world that either provided solace or a chance to run away. Some would argue that it stems from my anti-social nature and there's an element of truth in that. It's no wonder that Uncle Wal gave me a copy of Colin Wilson's *The Outsider* when I was 16. But let's return to when I was 11 years old and in my first days at Torquay Boys' Grammar School. I now had a uniform and new satchel and wearing long trousers meant I would no longer need zinc and castor oil cream to treat chapped legs in the winter. Isn't it odd how one remembers such things? The atmosphere at TBGS was formal and all the familiarity, inclusiveness and enjoyment of learning at Oldway Primary were changed. Masters wore gowns, were mostly rather severe, and learning was now a serious matter. I had embarked on the grim business of growing up.

Each subject was taught by a different Master and governed by a syllabus, as we needed to absorb information for national examinations. There was some rote learning but also problem solving and an introduction to many new topics. This was fascinating but I didn't have the confidence, or the inclination, to develop my interests beyond the material we covered in class and in homework. There was one exception and this was in Biology, where we now learned how organisms worked and how they were constructed. That spurred me into looking at encyclopaedias and books in the local Public Library, as well as those available in the school. It looked as though Biology was going to be my favourite subject.

If Biology was a strong positive, its negative counterpart was Games. I was no good at anything sporty, despite the hours of cricket and football played with friends and with my eldest brother David in Victoria Park and elsewhere. Games were football, rugby and cross country running in the winter; cricket and athletics during the summer. Swimming was held throughout the year and I hated that most of all. Although visits to the swimming bath meant a pleasant walk from the school to Torquay seafront, there was no possibility of enjoyment on the stroll, just the dread of what was to come. Making me jump into the pool was never going to make me overcome my fear of water and my dislike of school began when I was made to go to the swimming baths. My relief at having survived these lessons was always celebrated when I returned home by making a Cheese Dream, my version being a Cheddar cheese sandwich fried on both sides in lard. Clearly, Games didn't always promote healthy living.

Having jumped from the second year straight to the fourth at TBGS, I took eight Ordinary Level exams when I was 15 and passed in seven subjects. The only failure was in Biology, the subject in which I was most interested and expected to pass with a very high grade. This slip-up remains a mystery as I stayed until the end of the examination and certainly wrote an answer to each question. Perhaps in my enthusiasm I deviated from the topic too often? Fortunately, the failure did not prevent me from going on to take Advanced Levels in Botany, Zoology, Physics and Chemistry. We took both Botany and Zoology at the South Devon Technical College, in a building adjacent to TBGS. Teaching was shared between the two institutions, with Botany taught by Mr Hood from the Grammar School and Zoology by Mr Cosway from the Tech. The classes were mixed, both in the ability of the students and in the presence of both boys and girls. There were two girls, Vicki and Roxanne, and they were way out of my league. I remember being rather scared of them, as I'd not mixed with girls for four years – the penalty of having only brothers.

In Botany and Zoology we continued to learn about structure and function, but the syllabuses also required us to know about the classification of plants and animals and how to recognise a wide range of different types. A contemporary student of Biology would barely recognise the content of our courses, as they were anchored in the developments of the subject which underwent such an explosion in Victorian times. I took the examination in Botany after one year and failed (what was it about me and examinations in Biology?) so re-took it the following year, together with the rest of the Advanced Levels. A third year in the Sixth Form then resulted in yet more taking of examinations and mine was hardly a glowing academic record. Could events at home have affected me more than I realised at the time?

Neither of the two highlights of my academic efforts from these years involved the syllabus. The first was a plant survey on land attached to Paignton Zoo and the second the collection trips made with two fellow students to the rock pools at Corbyn's Head in Torquay. I always enjoyed visiting Paignton Zoo to gaze at the animals and I had joined the Peacock Association (the Friends of the Zoo) to gain free entry. On the south side of the Zoo was a private area behind a high double gate and that led to mature woodland and a hillside that was partly grazed by rabbits. Mr Hood had kept a record of the plants on the hillside over several years and a group of us Botany students was taken there to continue mapping the site using quadrats. It was something that happened with the class in each year and taught botanical surveying techniques. I really enjoyed this field work and my earlier flower collecting meant that I could identify many plants, although I now used Latin names rather than the common ones. I went back to the site on my own a few times and continued the survey in other areas and this impressed, and surprised, Mr Hood who, like Mr Cosway, didn't think I had much of a future academically. This was around the time of the worst phase of the Cold War between the West and Russia and I didn't know whether there would be a future at all, let alone an academic one. I remember carrying a Bible around with me on the day of Kennedy's ultimatum to Krushchev in the Cuban Missile Crisis and that showed how scared I was, and how my Christian roots still found expression during stressful times.

RSW (age 18) in his final year at Torquay Boys' Grammar School in 1965. Most of the time was spent at South Devon Technical College, or collecting at Corbyn's Head. (From Author's Collection).

I liked Mr Hood as he clearly loved plants and seemed independent-minded, although we only had occasional glimpses of the human side of our school Masters. He had spent time in India with the Army and was almost a caricature of someone from that background, having a large moustache and usually wearing a rumpled tweed sports jacket and cavalry twills. Occasionally, he talked to us about the Western Ghats and some of his Indian adventures and these seemed very alien, especially with my very limited experience of places other than Torbay. Mr Cosway was a quite different character. I'm not sure that he had ever taught in schools and he provided my first encounter with someone who had conducted research, having been awarded an MSc from the University of Birmingham. He knew a lot about Zoology and gave us a good grounding in the academic subject, but there was no Natural History and little joy. Perhaps that was why three of us went collecting on the rocky shore below Corbyn's Head in Torquay. As we were spending half of our week at South Devon Tech., we had the freedom to do this, instead of being in the library at the Grammar School as regulations demanded. We collected material in buckets to bring to aquarium tanks at the School and kept a wide range of organisms alive for weeks in them. Even though the Biology teaching staff showed them to students from classes lower down the School, that wasn't enough to save us. Our truancy was discovered and we were told to discontinue the collecting trips.

The identification of plants and animals in our collections was aided by *Collins' Pocket Guide to the Sea Shore*,[1] which had simple keys and many illustrations produced by a team of seven artists. Mine was a 1958 first edition bought second hand, and, in addition to its use as a field guide and means of identification, it was an opening into another world and I was now determined to become a field biologist of some sort. With hindsight, all my earlier experiences of coast and country in Devon were pointing in this direction.

Leaving home for University

After the three years of trying, I managed to get just enough Advanced Level grades to gain a place at Reading University. I will always remember Gramp's comment when I raced to his house and told him I had been given a place. His initial reaction showed that he was either pleased, and couldn't express it, or that he was amazed that such a thing could happen. He asked me what I was going to do that evening and I said I might go to the pub and have a pint of beer, a very rare event for me in those days. 'You wouldn't do that if your mother was still alive' was his reply. Victorian Christian values indeed.

Reading had a strong reputation in both Marine and Freshwater Biology, and also offered a good all-round education in Zoology, my chosen programme. At University, academics could teach what they wanted, rather than some fixed syllabus, and I was carried along by this new approach and the enthusiasm of so many different lecturers. Zoology retained the classical approach with which I had become familiar and we spent the first year learning about invertebrate and vertebrate structure and function. Lectures were accompanied by weekly dissection classes where, just as at Advanced Level, we had to make detailed drawings to aid our observations. I was rather good at this, despite my lack of talent as an artist, and always managed an accurate representation and good labels. The lazy, half-hearted approach I was content with at South Devon Tech. had now changed to one of greater commitment.

The Department of Zoology, and the University as a whole, were friendly which was important to someone as insecure as myself. Moving to Reading not only took me away from the bad learning habits acquired at the Tech. but also away from home and thus the responsibility of having to prevent the worst effects of my father's illness. With the last of his children now leaving, Dad must have felt very alone in our large, cold house with its coal fire and single electric fan heater. On the other hand, he would have been relieved that his most difficult son was now away for ten weeks at a time. I think it must have been trying for him to have a surly adolescent around who agreed with little that he believed in and yet required a lot of support financially and in day-to-day life. Like any loving father, he came to visit me once I had settled in at University and I was proud to show him around and, having done that, I left him in his hotel. This was cruel and I regret it deeply now. At the time, I suppose it was a selfish way of expressing my transition to independence.

Of course, my shyness stayed with me through University and I found approaching people difficult, although the student community made it much easier, as there are few environments where it is so easy to mix. Talking casually with fellow students was fine, but attempting to get a girlfriend was much more problematic. I went to dances in the Great Hall but these filled me with dread, as approaching girls usually required more courage than I possessed. Oh, for the happy days of organised Country Dancing at Oldway Primary. I was hijacked by my first girlfriend, having been introduced to her as one of a group. She decided she would make a move and, of course, I was a pushover. Then, in my second year at Reading I met my first serious girlfriend and I don't recall how things progressed from chatting to kissing. I thought she was wonderful and it was all puppy love on my side, I'm sure. We went out on and off for two years, but because of my upbringing and insecurities it made me too possessive and I couldn't think of our relationship as being casual. Inevitably, I was ditched and it hurt. It was just something I had to live with as there were no emotional props and my religious feelings were focussed in a strong anti-Christianity at that time. Indeed, one of the Christian Union visitors who knocked at my room was so taken aback by my responses to his probing questions that he told me I was the closest he had ever come to the Devil. This comment felt good at the time but it is another incident of which I'm not very proud; one which came from a growing self-belief in amongst the fear. I wince mentally when thinking about it now and hope that I am no longer guilty of that type of behaviour.

So I had a strong side, but it ran in parallel with the anxious me, which now started to show in psychosomatic symptoms. Lecture theatres gave me a feeling of being trapped and I would get an urgent feeling that I needed a pee. Not knowing anything about the symptoms of anxiety, or what anxiety was as a medical condition, I didn't confide in anyone. I felt that it was some unfortunate problem unique to me, and classmates must have been puzzled by my occasional wriggling and leg-crossing. It wasn't funny at the time and my concentration was certainly affected, but I never walked out.

Although I went back home from Reading for vacations,

I was happier at University, where I was becoming absorbed more and more by Zoology. It was easy to get back to Paignton by train and I sent my large suitcase by advanced freight. That meant I could carry my record player, LPs and a few personal things to, and from, the railway stations. Now that we have MP3s, it is difficult to remember just how heavy a collection of vinyl records could be, but my travel arrangements meant that I always had my LPs of Elgar, Vaughan Williams and all the works of Bob Dylan with me. Dad didn't mind some of the popular Elgar tunes, but he struggled with Bob Dylan and that was a problem as I was becoming a very big fan. My singing along, with full nasal intonation, must have been agony to hear: 'How does it feel, how does it feel, to be on your own ...' Outside the house, days in Paignton during vacations were spent walking, wandering around the coast and continuing with the activities that I had always enjoyed. Occasionally, my girlfriend would come to visit but most of our contact away from Reading was by letter. It seems so strange now, given the many means of instant communication like texts, e-mail and Facebook.

On a field course from Reading University held in North Wales (1966).
RSW second left (age 19). (From Author's Collection).

The Zoology degree programme included a small research project during the summer vacation of the second year. Some sensible fellow students organised placements at laboratories where they joined existing research programmes, gaining a head-start on those of us who worked on our own. By now, I had developed a passion for Freshwater Biology, and especially for dragonflies, so was determined to organise a project that would enable me to discover more about these insects. The 'New Naturalist' book on dragonflies by Corbet, Longfield and Moore provided a starting point (what a brilliant series of books that was for inspiring inexperienced Natural Historians) and that was followed by research papers on the behaviour and distribution of dragonflies and damselflies. But what was I to investigate in the project? I had an academic supervisor back in Reading but he did not help much in planning and certainly not in selecting suitable field sites.

I contacted Leslie Jackman for advice. In addition to his roles as teacher, museum officer, broadcaster and aquarium owner, he made films for the BBC Natural History Unit series called *Look*.[2] Mr Jackman was filming at some ponds near Newton Abbot and I went with him to prospect these as a possible location for my project work. Fortunately, the ponds were ideal and I then identified dragonflies and damselflies, assessed their territorial behaviour, and monitored their population changes over time. It was pretty feeble science, but a very enjoyable experience. The resulting project report, which bore little resemblance to a scientific paper, was handed in on my return to Reading at the end of the vacation and, as we were not told our marks, I have no idea how well the report was received. The bonus for me in being in touch with Mr Jackman was that I was able to help in filming. The programme he was making was called 'Town Mouse and Country Mouse' (or something like that), so it was nothing to do with dragonflies. He was filming the location shots at the ponds near Newton Abbot, much of the detailed camera work being completed in a shed at the bottom of his garden. It was fun to slide a mouse through a clear plastic tube into an aquarium tank and know that the impression given in the final film was of the same mouse having been filmed by chance at the moment it dived into a pond.

In my final year came the realisation that this happy student life would stop and I began to think about continuing in research. From school days I had always thought of Canada as an interesting country and remember taking out books from the Public Library to find out more. There was something about the scenic grandeur, the wilderness and the size of the country which appealed to me and I now had the idea of going to Canada to study for a PhD. With the support of one of my lecturers, I wrote to entomologists, especially to those interested in dragonflies, and was offered places subject to funding being available, but in the end I chickened out. I don't think I had the confidence to set off on my own and I was also concerned about Dad. This concern was behind much of my anxiety at the time, I now realise. An opportunity came up at the University of Salford so I went there, and that is why I was in Manchester when I received the news that Dad had died.

Although I was now an embryo Freshwater Biologist, I continued to make visits to the sea shore in Torbay to look at rock pools. This ended when we sold the family home and the demands of research meant that there were no more long vacations with spare time. The *Collins Guide* was always the first place I looked for help with identification but, by now, I was reading scientific research papers avidly, so it was a natural step to consult the bibliography of the book to get further information on different organisms. Under the heading 'Coelenterates' was the following entry: '*A History of British Sea Anemones and Corals* by P. H. Gosse (Van Voorst 1860) remains a classic work on sea anemones. Has excellent colour illustrations.' I didn't look out a copy of this work as it seemed so old, even though it was referenced in the Guide. Unbeknown to me at the time, this was my first contact with Henry Gosse and his work. I now realise what an important figure he was in the development of Natural History and the way we view the natural world.

1 Barrett, J. H., and Yonge, C. M., (1958) *Collins Pocket Guide to the Sea Shore*, (Collins), London, 1958.

2 For the development, history and programmes of the BBC National History Unit see http:// en.wikipedia.org/wiki/BBC_Natural_History_Unit Note the reference to Leslie Jackman in this citation.

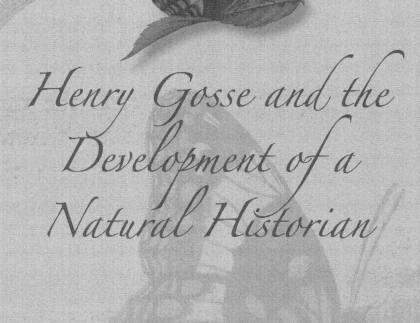

Henry Gosse and the Development of a Natural Historian

Henry Gosse, The Aquarium and looking through microscopes

The following pages I have endeavoured, as far as possible, to make a mirror of the thoughts and feelings that have occupied my own mind during a nine months' residence on the charming shores of North and South Devon. There I have been pursuing an occupation which always possesses for me new delight, - the study of the curious forms, and still more curious instincts, of animated beings. So interesting, so attractive has the pursuit been, so unexpected in many instances the facts revealed by the research, that I have thought the attempt to convey, with pen and pencil, to others the impressions vividly received by myself might be a welcome service.

Few, very few, are at all aware of the many strange, beautiful, or wondrous objects that are to be found by searching on those shores that every season are crowded by idle pleasure-seekers. Most curious and interesting animals are dwelling within a few yards of your feet, whose lovely forms and hues, exquisitely contrived structures, and amusing instincts, could not fail to attract and charm your attention, if you were once cognizant of them.

From the Preface of *A Naturalist's Rambles on the Devonshire Coast*
by Philip Henry Gosse.

When looking at the contents of the tanks we set up in Torquay Boys' Grammar School, or of those in Paignton Aquarium, I didn't know anything of the history of aquaria and their use in allowing us to observe living aquatic creatures. I knew a little more about the development of microscopes and this stemmed from my reading after we were given the small instrument by Gramp. I could not have studied Botany and Zoology without the aid of a microscope and we had a number of old brass instruments at school and at University, giving an insight into microscopy of earlier times.

Henry Gosse was an enthusiast for both aquaria and microscopes, and wrote books to encourage their use for looking at living organisms. Of course, his audience was the Victorians who owned villas and town houses, not the majority of the population, who could not afford such luxuries. It was this audience that made Henry famous; and it was the members of this stratum in society who were the explorers, adventurers and collectors of the day and who relished the opportunities given by the power and wealth of the Empire. The majority of people in Britain were involved in making money for this élite, who were increasing in numbers and interested, then as now, in keeping up with new trends. Aquaria and microscopes were part of that desire for status but also more than just that. Both provided a means of exploring unknown worlds from within the parlour.

Gosse is regarded as the inventor of the modern aquarium and his experiments with aeration and water flow allowed long-term survival of aquatic organisms in small containers for the first time. Remember, this is before electric pumps and it was only in the mid-nineteenth century that sheet glass was manufactured in sufficient quantity to allow the construction of the aquarium tanks we know today. Visitors to modern large-scale aquaria are able to walk through huge tanks to get a 3-D view of fish and invertebrates, but seeing what resided below the surface of the sea was a novelty 150 years ago. We need to transport ourselves back in time to appreciate the effect that aquaria had on members of the public.

Gosse wrote about marine vivaria (later to be termed aquaria) in *A Naturalists' Rambles on the Devonshire Coast*, [1] describing one of his early versions as a confectionary jar '10 inches deep by 5½ inches wide, [having] about three pints of sea-water, and some marine plants and animals.' He topped up the level of the water to overcome evaporation and no animals died in nearly two months, the water remaining clear, with only a 'slight floccose yellow deposition' on the sides of the jar. Later in the same book, Henry writes that he was able to keep sea anemones alive in marine vivaria in London, providing there was sufficient light to support oxygenation of the water by algae. Nevertheless, mucus from the anemones, together with decaying plants, began to decompose and give off a bad smell, especially when the water was moved and sediments disturbed. This problem was solved by aerating the water by 'passing it through the air in a slender stream' and then decomposition in the absence of air did not occur, for it was this that had caused the production of smelly gases.

Robert Warington, the Chemical Operator of the Society of Apothecaries, was also developing aquaria at the time [2] and had designed one for freshwater organisms. Henry was in contact with Warington and brought him some marine creatures so that he could also set up a sea water version. There was no rivalry between the two enthusiasts and Gosse acknowledged that the aquarium was not his invention alone but, nevertheless, it was Henry Gosse who popularised aquaria and who also developed the most famous public aquaria of the day. Henry tells his readers that, to see an aquarium in action, they should visit the Zoological Gardens in Regent's Park where a large plate glass tank contained many invertebrates 'enjoying themselves without restraint'. Seven further tanks were planned to join the original and make a most impressive exhibit. Henry collected organisms for the Regent's Park aquarium when living in Weymouth and these were sent off in bags of seaweed to ensure oxygenation and thus good survival. Animals were collected both from the shore and from deeper areas, as Gosse was also a pioneer in the use of dredging from boats to collect animals.

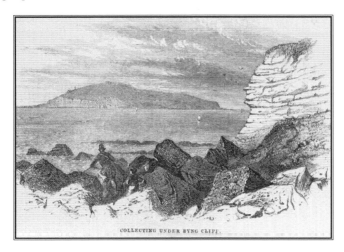

'Collecting under Byng Cliff.'
From *The Aquarium: an unveiling of the wonders of the deep sea.*
Byng Cliff is near Weymouth.

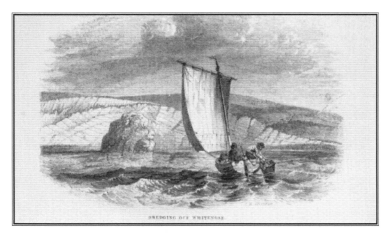

Dredging for specimens.
From *The Aquarium: an unveiling of the wonders of the deep sea.*

Living creatures were also provided for an aquarium at Crystal Palace, but this did not please the Zoological Society, where the Council became defensive when faced with this rival attraction. Gosse had not been acknowledged by the Society at their exhibit in Regent's Park and this, together with their view of exclusivity (which had never been agreed), meant that he stopped supplying them with material. The Council had clearly acted in a high-handed manner and it is amusing to note that, in celebrating the bicentenary of the birth of Gosse in April 2010, the Zoological Society of London acknowledges that 'Gosse was instrumental in the establishment of London Zoo's "Fish House", ZSL's first Aquarium.' It's good to see that the contemporary members of the Council do not behave in the same way as their haughty predecessors and that the Society duly acknowledged Gosse's major contribution, albeit over 150 years too late.

Although upset by these events, Henry turned to the development of small 'parlour' aquaria for entertainment in the home. Gosse saw these as a means of making money to support himself, as he had little income apart from the sale of books. In September 1853, he began work on *The Aquarium*, subtitled an *unveiling of the wonders of the deep sea*. [3] Most of the work consists of enthusiastic, detailed and accurate descriptions of organisms that can be observed readily. A final chapter gives details both for construction of an aquarium and on maintaining and stocking it. Perhaps the best way of showing Gosse's enthusiasm and knowledge of the subject is to quote sections from the Preface of the book:

The habits of animals will never be thoroughly known till they are observed in detail. Nor is it sufficient to mark them with attention now and then; they must be closely watched, their various actions carefully noted, their behaviour under different circumstances, and especially those movements which seem to us mere vagaries, undirected by any suggestive motive or cause, well examined... The most interesting parts, by far, of published natural history, are those minute, but most graphic particulars, which have been gathered by an attentive watching of individual animals... A paragraph went round the papers some months ago, to the effect that an eminent French zoologist, in order to prosecute his studies on the marine animals of the Mediterranean, had provided himself with a water-tight dress, suitable spectacles, and a breathing-tube; so that he might walk on the bottom in a considerable depth of water, and mark the habits of the various creatures pursuing their avocations... Whether a scheme so elaborate was really attempted I know not; but I should anticipate feeble results from it. The MARINE AQUARIUM, however, bids fair to supply the required opportunities, and to make us acquainted with the strange creatures of the sea, without diving to gaze on them... The following pages embrace a brief History of the Marine Aquarium, as an application of scientific principles to a definite object;-my own Experience in collecting animals and plants, with Instructions founded thereon;-copious Details of the peculiar habits and instincts of such species as I have observed in confinement;-Sketches of scenery, of local customs and manners, and of personal adventure, made during the prosecution of the employment; and, finally, an arranged chapter of Directions for the construction, preparation, stocking, and maintenance of a Marine Aquarium.

The final chapter referred to in the last paragraph of this quotation contains a description of everything needed by the amateur aquarist, including the design of tanks of various kinds and how to prepare an aquarium for its inhabitants. It is recommended that water for a marine aquarium is best obtained by paying the master, or steward, of a sea-going vessel to dip a cask into the sea beyond the influence of rivers, the cask not having previously contained any harmful chemicals. Ever thoughtful and well-researched, Henry also gives a recipe for artificial sea water, should natural water not be available. There follow a further thirty pages on stocking the aquarium and the various methods of collection from the sea shore and from further out at sea. Many enthusiasts must have been grateful for this detailed advice and instruction when embarking on their new hobby or parlour entertainment.

As *The Aquarium* was expensive at 17 shillings, the final chapter was expanded and published separately a year later as *A Handbook to the Marine Aquarium*, selling for 2 shillings and 6 pence. [4] Both books were successful and amongst Henry's best-selling works, and Freeman and Wertheimer in the scholarly *Philip Henry Gosse: A Bibliography*, [5] report that Henry received more than £650 in income from the two. Given so much information, readers of both books must have been very keen to get started and also to visit Regent's Park, or Crystal Palace, to see what could be done on a larger scale, should they be ambitious.

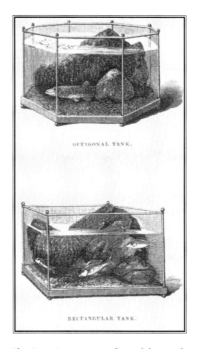

Illustration from *The Aquarium: an unveiling of the wonders of the deep sea.*

Development of aquaria did not stop there. Later in life, Henry built an aquarium with a circulating water system at his house in St Marychurch, Torquay. A slate reservoir (of capacity 210 gallons) was sunk into the garden next to the house and this was connected to a slate cistern on the roof of the kitchen (of capacity 120 gallons), the two being linked by vulcanite pipes and a glass pump. Once a week, an hour's pumping replenished the cistern which drained 17 gallons of water a day into the show tank (capacity 50 gallons). This was also made of slate but had a plate glass viewing window. Water entered as a jet to ensure oxygenation and the circuit was completed by a tube draining from the base of the show tank back to the reservoir. Henry was in his mid-sixties when this aquarium was set up and it must have required some effort, and many walks to the shore, to collect all the water necessary and then pump it from the reservoir to the roof cistern on a regular basis.

Moving forward a century or more, our aquaria at Torquay Boys' Grammar School would certainly have benefitted from Gosse's information, if only we had been aware of it. Of course, we had the luxury of electric aquarium pumps to allow aeration, but Henry's background knowledge on maintaining aquatic communities would have been invaluable. We would also have welcomed him on our illicit trips to Corbyn's Head and enjoyed his meticulous descriptions of animals and plants and the obvious satisfaction that their study brought him.

Rocks at Corbyn's Head, where RSW and PHG collected from pools.
(From Author's Collection).

Like all students of Botany and Zoology, from Victorian times through to twenty years ago, we spent a lot of time as Advanced Level and undergraduate students looking down microscopes, both at pre-prepared slides and those we had made ourselves. There was fun to be had in cutting sections through plants, staining them with dyes such as eosin and haematoxylin, and seeing the result; or using similar approaches to see the structure of animal tissues. Of course, it was not just fun for we learned more about organisms this way.

Microscopy was becoming a popular occupation in wealthier Victorian households and brass microscopes were not just scientific instruments but for entertainment after dinner. They were also beautiful objects that could be admired by visitors. In *Edmund Gosse: A Literary Landscape*, [6] Ann Thwaite relates that Henry Gosse bought a copy of *Adams's Essays on the Microscope* in an auction on 5 May 1832, but it was seventeen years later that he acquired a microscope. There was much to see with this absorbing instrument and Henry followed his book *The Aquarium: an unveiling of the wonders of the deep sea* with *Evenings at the Microscope; or researches among the minuter forms of animal life* [7] which Freeman and Wertheimer describe as one of Henry's most successful books, remaining in print until 1905 – some 46 years. It consists of descriptions of various parts of animals that can be viewed under the microscope, with many illustrations to help the reader. It goes far beyond my own rather feeble efforts in microscopy and one can grasp the sense of wonder that Henry felt looking at all the animals, and parts of animals, described. It was the result of many hours of work, some for pleasure and some also for developing Henry's research interest on insects and rotifers ('wheel animalcules'), both of which are given sections in the book. My favourite example comes in the description of a hydroid attached to the rim of the tube of the marine fan worm *Sabella*. This hydroid has two tentacles and a constriction behind the oral region. Called *Lar* in the book, each hydroid looks just like a miniature human body, with head and two outstretched arms:

This clear terminal portion of the tube you may perceive to be occupied by a curious parasite. About twenty bodies, having a most ludicrously-close resemblance to the human figure, and as closely imitating certain human motions, are seen standing erect around the mouth of the tube, now that the *Sabella* has retired into the interior, and are incessantly bowing and tossing about their arms in the most energetic manner.

The description is accompanied by one of Henry's drawings, that really does appear to show graceful forms in movement (the drawing could also pass for an art deco work).

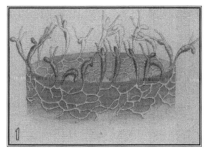

FIGURE 1.
A reproduction of Gosse's (1857) figure of *Lar sabellarum* on the extremity of a tube of *Sabella vesiculosa* (*Trans. Linnean Soc.* 22: 113-116).

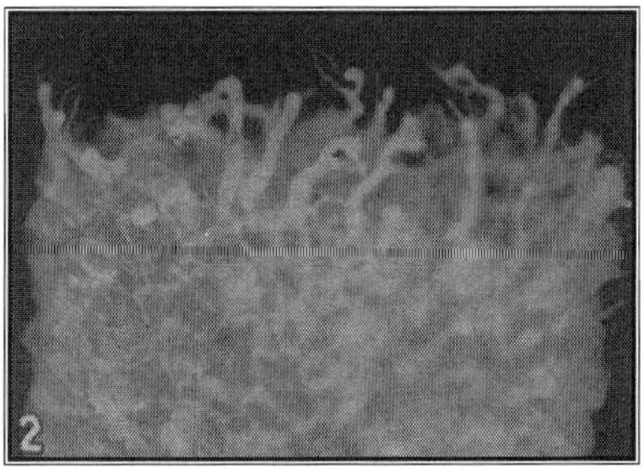

FIGURE 2.
A living colony of *Proboscidactyla* sp. on a tube of *Pseudopotamilla ocellata* (ca. 25 x) from Hand and Hendrickson (1950, *Biol. Bull.* 99: 74-87).

(Both reprinted with permission from the Marine Biological Laboratory, Woods Hole, MA)

This illustration was repeated nearly a hundred years later in 1950 in a paper by Hand and Hendrickson in volume 99 of the *Biological Bulletin*, [8] describing the animal and other, similar commensals. Adjacent to the illustration is a photograph of a related hydroid also living at the entrance to a tube, showing that Henry's drawing and description were based on very accurate observation.

One can imagine how readers reacted to his drawing and some may have been captivated by the anthropomorphic similarities, rather than the more detached series of descriptions that Henry had made. He was a great observer of Nature and had the happy ability to write very well and communicate detail with enthusiasm.

Henry Gosse's early life and the development of his interest in Natural History

So what was Henry Gosse's background and how did his interest in Natural History develop? We have a record of Henry's early life in his son Edmund's biography *The Naturalist of the Sea-Shore: The Life of Philip Henry Gosse*, [9] published in 1890. As this first biography was written soon after Henry died, I take it to be an accurate chronological and historical record of Henry's work as a Natural Historian, although I might be mistaken. Without any controversy, it is clear that Henry's interest in Natural History developed early and it is easy for me to empathise with that.

Henry Gosse was born on 6 April 1810 above Garner's shoemakers shop in High Street, Worcester (the same street where another great Englishman, Edward Elgar, lived for much of his childhood fifty years later). Henry's father, Thomas Gosse was an artist, a lover of poetry and a romantic who had trained at the Royal Academy Schools. In her biography of Edmund Gosse, Ann Thwaite tells us that Thomas was taught at the Royal Academy by Sir Joshua Reynolds, a fellow pupil at the time being William Blake, although it is not known whether the two had much contact. Thomas became an engraver and itinerant artist, travelling the country seeking commissions for the miniatures in which he specialised, although he didn't have much 'push'.

Henry's mother, Hannah Best, was one of Thomas's muses and the daughter of a bullying mother from whom she had run away. Hannah was certainly not a romantic by nature and she was the ever-present parent, as Thomas was away from home for long periods. Henry was the second child, the other children being William (b.1808), Elizabeth (b.1813) and Thomas (b. 1816).

Henry's paternal grandfather, William Gosse, was a wealthy cloth manufacturer who had twelve children, Thomas being the eleventh. He had been the High Sherriff of Radnorshire and thus had high status, although this was to change when machinery for processing wool was invented, resulting in hard times financially for his company. William's fourth child, Susan ('Aunt Bell') was an important influence on Henry and nurtured his interest in Natural History. Aunt Bell lived in Poole, as did two of her sisters, and Hannah Gosse moved to the town and settled there while Thomas continued his nomadic life. Aunt Bell was married to a surgeon and her interest in animals and plants was conveyed both to Henry and to her own son Thomas who was to become a distinguished zoologist and a Fellow of the Royal Society. Aunt Bell had been a teacher and she collected animals from the shore, a practice which clearly inspired Henry.

As a child, Henry was bookish and clever. He suffered from 'morbid bashfulness', an old-fashioned term for the shyness with which I am certainly familiar, and he had one close friend, John Hammond Brown, who shared his interests in Natural History and in books. They were 'inseparable companions from morning to night.' Fortunately, Henry and John were sent to school together in Blandford, but Henry returned to Poole early to become a clerk in a company trading with Newfoundland. John came back to Poole after further schooling and the two boys were again inseparable, the friendship lasting until 1827 when Henry was offered a six-year contract to work in the counting house of Elson's, a company in Newfoundland. Quite a change for a 17-year old, but his elder brother William had preceded him in taking the big step of moving across the Atlantic.

It was a time of expansion and discovery for British trade and there was a general spirit of adventure for those in a position to seek employment abroad, especially from families with aspirations and a sense of importance. Henry was reluctant to go, but his stern mother insisted that he take the position. She probably viewed it both as a way of increasing Henry's prospects and as a means of encouraging another son to take the natural step of leaving home, but it was a frightening prospect for someone of Henry's psychological make-up. Six years is a long time for a very young man to contemplate and not remotely like going to University for three years as we do today, with the chance of frequent return visits home and a developed support system in place. Even with William nearby, Henry was on his own, and communication with home would only be by occasional letters carried across the Atlantic by ships. It accentuated the feeling of remoteness.

Henry sailed for Newfoundland on the brig *Carbonear*, the name of the vessel being appropriate as that was the name of the town to which they were heading. Winds were against them almost all the way across the Atlantic and the voyage lasted 46 days, a long time to be at sea with uncertain weather conditions and without much to observe. There were only three other passengers on the crossing, one of whom was 15 years old, but the two young men were made very much part of shipboard life. Henry was not affected as much by his shyness in such a small group, and his liking for jokes must have made him a good travelling companion. To quote Ann Thwaite, Henry was not 'pious or priggish' at this stage in his life, although he did follow his mother's request that he should read his Bible daily. Whilst time did not pass quickly, Henry had much to occupy him as there was a diary to write on the journey and books about the natural world to read so the two mainstays of his life were firmly in place: The Bible and Natural History.

The welcoming party on arrival at Carbonear included Henry's brother William, so there was a familiar face to greet him. He settled in to his lodgings and began work at the counting house where a fellow clerk was William Charles St. John (Charley), the two becoming close friends, just as John and Henry had been in Dorset. Charley lived in Harbour Grace, near Carbonear, and was brought up in Newfoundland, so the colony was home to him. Their shared interests, inevitably, were in Natural History and in reading books, and Charley was also a poet, reinforcing the love of poetry and words that Henry had received from his father. The two youths enjoyed lively discussions and the replacement of John by Charley was reassuring for Henry. The friendship, together with the presence of William nearby, meant that he could throw himself into his new life without the likelihood of too much homesickness.

In 1828, Mr Elson posted Henry to St Mary's, a small fishing town along the coast that felt even more remote than Carbonear. He lived in a room over the office and this added to the feeling of isolation. The manager at St Mary's, John Martin, was coincidentally from Poole, but the relationship between the two was not a happy one as Martin liked to intimidate Henry. Sundays brought relief from the tensions of work and freedom from all contact with Elson's. Then, Henry explored the surrounding bleak countryside on solitary walks, a good means of discovering any local area, as I found many years later. On occasions, he visited William Phippard and his family. William was a merchant in St. Mary's and his daughter Emma became Henry's closest friend, replacing Charley in that role. We don't know if there was any romantic attachment in Henry's mind, and we don't know Emma's age, but his days off were not devoid of company.

After a year at St Mary's, Henry was summoned to return to Carbonear on foot, partly in the company of a trapper, Joe, from whom he learned about survival skills and who had many fascinating tales of wildlife. It was exciting to hear of how to capture animals and to gain a trapper's insight into the behaviour of different species and the way they reacted to seasons. There was also an introduction to practical skills like bush cooking; delicious roast beaver being a lasting memory for Henry of his encounter with Joe. After parting from the trapper, Henry walked on and arrived at Harbour Grace to a warm welcome from the hospitable St John family, and Charley and Henry then talked through the night, as there was much news to tell. Recent trapper tales no doubt featured strongly in their conversation and Joe, with his free way of life, made a strong impression on the sensitive youth. Henry was bursting to share his impressions with Charley but this was to be one of the last times they met as close friends. Not long after Henry's return to Carbonear, Charley married and their friendship inevitably changed.

Bad news came from Poole in 1832, as Henry's sister Elizabeth had become seriously ill and he was very concerned, especially as he had no way of knowing her present condition. Mr Elson advised an immediate return to England on the next available ship, due to leave in a few weeks and Henry sailed from Carbonear on 10 July, arriving in Poole on 6 August. It was a more rapid crossing than he had endured travelling west and that must have brought some comfort, although it was still a long time without news. After disembarking, he went straight to Skinner Street, knocked at the door of his old home and was very relieved to hear that Elizabeth was recovering well. This excellent news brought a happy frame of mind and Henry was now free to spend his time in Dorset collecting insects from the local area. He departed once again for Carbonear on 20 September, having spent seven weeks in Poole and the surrounding region. A fascination with the natural world was now coupled to Henry's drive and persistence and he began the life of a committed Natural Historian that was to continue for the rest of his life.

On return to Newfoundland, Henry was promoted and his work in the office now consisted of copying ledgers, something that was not demanding and which left time and energy for insect collection. A sea captain had brought Henry a collector's cabinet from Hamburg, made to strict instructions, and this now housed expanding numbers of preserved and pinned insects. As no-one had made a systematic collection of insects in Newfoundland, Henry was the pioneer and this was an added incentive, yet his life didn't only revolve around work and collecting insects, as time was also spent with new friends, a young couple called Mr and Mrs Jaques. Unfortunately, they were not prospering in Newfoundland and, as a result, the Jaques' decided to move to Upper Canada and try farming. By now, Henry had stayed on beyond the end of his agreement with Elson and he decided to go with the Jaques, as another worker on the farm would be very welcome and the friendship was close.

The three sailed on the *Camilla* from Harbour Grace in June 1835, together with the immature stages of butterflies 'the premature transformation of some of which gave him a great deal of anxiety.' Landing at Quebec, the three journeyed by open carriage to Compton, viewed a partially cleared farm and bought it on impulse. Of course, the viewing was in summer when the prospect of farming was greeted with enthusiasm and the three were all naive pioneers. It was a common attitude of the time, but their enthusiasm didn't last long as Mrs Jaques quickly tired of housekeeping and there was also a young baby to look after. She was used to the life of a gentlewoman, so the long hours and routine of a farmer's wife soon wore her down. Henry and Mr Jaques also tired of the project as they found the farm work difficult and there was so much to do, as not all the land had been cleared. According to Edmund, it was only the study of insects that kept Henry going at this time and a key support was provided by membership of both the Literary and Historical Society of Quebec and the Natural History Society of Montreal. These Societies not only gave Henry a sense of worth but he began publishing in their journals on insects he had found and on the local climate. After three years, Henry decided that he had had enough of the farm and left, even though the friendship of Mr and Mrs Jaques was very important to him. They parted on good terms.

Henry set out on 22 March 1838 for a passage to the United States, hoping, in time, to reach the southern states of Georgia and the Carolinas for further studies of Natural History. The first part of the journey was in the company of Mr Jaques who drove them in his open wagon but it was not smooth going and the Hamburg insect cabinet, crammed with pinned specimens was badly broken, leaving Henry in a state 'of misery beyond speech or tears.' They drove together into New England and Mr Jaques then departed back from Burlington, where Henry boarded a southbound stagecoach. By 26 March he had reached Philadelphia and met with Titian Peale, 'a local zoological artist of considerable eminence', who was impressed by the drawings of insects that Henry had made. Another new acquaintance was Professor Thomas Nuttal who invited Henry to the Academy of Natural Sciences to meet a number of fellow enthusiasts, amongst which was Timothy A. Conrad, a conchologist, who suggested that Alabama would be a suitable destination for Henry to continue his work and provided him with a letter of introduction. Henry's obvious passion as a collector, and the skills as an artist he had learned from his father, enabled him to break through his shyness and make these valuable contacts.

The next part of the journey started on 18 April when Henry sailed on the *White Oak* bound for Mobile. He was the only passenger and had a rather miserable time, as conditions on board the ship were poor. There was a chance to observe marine organisms, however, and Henry dragged up some floating weed off Savannah to examine it. Later in the passage, some of the crew speared remoras in the Gulf of Mexico and they also landed a *Coryphaena* (a dolphinfish, described incorrectly as a dolphin by Edmund). Then there was a run through the cays linking Florida with the West Indies, where Henry was able to see the many colours of subtropical shallow seas. The long passage thus had some good experiences and the ship docked in Mobile on 14 May. Henry was apprehensive about what he might find and soon realised there was nothing in Mobile to occupy him, so he departed on a steamship passing up the Alabama River to King's Landing, a fellow passenger on this voyage being Hon. Chief Justice Reuben Saffold. By good luck, he offered Henry the job of local schoolmaster at Dallas, some 10 miles from King's Landing and where Saffold had a large house. The letter from Conrad in Philadelphia provided a reference.

There was much of interest in the flora and fauna of the South but Henry felt uncomfortable with the frontier-spirit lawlessness of the region. He was also confronted with slavery for the first time and felt physically ill when witnessing the brutal corporal punishment used on slaves while cotton picking. The atmosphere in Alabama was quite a change from anything he had experienced before and Henry recorded what he saw and felt in many diary entries. These ceased in early October and there were very few for the last three months he spent in Alabama, a time when Henry became ill with severe and persistent headaches which were probably psychosomatic in origin, caused by his concern and anxiety for all he witnessed. It was a type of illness that was to dog him for the rest of his life.

Henry had had enough and decided to leave Dallas, so packed up and headed back to Mobile where he was re-united with the Hamburg insect cabinet and found, to his surprise, that many of the insects were not damaged as badly as first thought during the rough treatment meted out by Mr Jaques' wagon. The cabinet remained in a sorry state after being left in a warehouse, but having the collection back pleased Henry very much.

Illustration of a beetle *Oryctes maimon* from *Letters from Alabama*.
(Reproduced with permission of the Zoological Society of London).

He set sail for England on the *Isaac Newton* in January 1839, having spent less than a year in Alabama, and arrived in Liverpool, staying with relatives of the Jaques' and raised money by selling some of the insects, pelts and rare bird skins that had been collected on his travels. He was writing a book, *The Canadian Naturalist*, that was based on his journal, and on which he had been working irregularly since his time there. Henry's writing continued after he moved to Wimborne in Dorset. Here, he supported himself with the fees he was given for teaching flower painting and those he earned for preaching in the place of absent ministers. Henry then set off for London but he was so poor that his meals consisted typically of a herring, every mouthful being savoured. His only friend at the time was his cousin Thomas Bell but that contact was to prove invaluable, as Bell read *The Canadian Naturalist* and recommended it to Van Voorst for publication. After reading the manuscript, Van Voorst accepted the book for 100 guineas and this news so pleased Henry that he broke into sobs. Thanks to the introduction made by his cousin, he was now to be the author of a Natural History book and a new career was possible. Given his current circumstances it is no wonder he sobbed with joy. He was an emotional man, even though these emotions were often strongly suppressed.

Philip Henry Gosse aged 29.
(With permission of the National Portrait Gallery)

Henry Gosse becomes a professional Natural Historian and writer

The Canadian Naturalist was published on 29 February 1840 and it set the tone for many of Henry's subsequent books. Although he was familiar with classification and morphology, his approach was not that of an academic, but of someone with an enthusiastic and open appreciation of plants and animals in their natural surroundings. He had a happy knack of being able to communicate his enthusiasm in words and, in reading his books, it is difficult not to feel that one is in the company of an author who has great energy and powers of observation and is eager to pass on knowledge of what he observes.

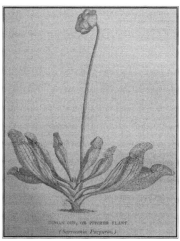

(Left) Larva, pupa and imago of the Banded Purple (*Limenitis arthemis*); (Right) Indian Cup, or Pitcher Plant (*Sarracenia purpurea*), from *The Canadian Naturalist*. (Reproduced with permission of the Zoological Society of London).

Perhaps because of his natural reticence, Henry did not promote himself using the popularity of *The Canadian Naturalist*, and spent his time teaching, drawing flowers and visiting museums to make sketches of various specimens. His dingy lodgings and surroundings in London depressed him and his thoughts turned time and again to the beautiful landscapes of Newfoundland, for he was primarily a countryman. On 26 July 1840 his sister Elizabeth, whose serious illness caused him to return from Newfoundland in 1832, died and this brought even more unhappiness. Something had to be done to overcome this gloomy phase and Henry decided to open a 'Classical and Commercial School for Young Gentlemen', taking over premises and three pupils in Hackney.

Using his own approach to tutoring, he was an excellent teacher and he moved to a small cottage to be near the school, his mother joining him there to act as housekeeper. The school did well for a time but, by the end of 1843, it had just eight pupils and Henry decided to take up another opportunity. The Society for Promoting Christian Knowledge (SPCK) wanted to publish two volumes on Zoology and a member of the 'Committee of General Literature and Education, Appointed by the Society for Promoting Christian Knowledge' suggested Henry as a suitable author. Thomas Bell, who was a member of this committee, consulted Van Voorst, and agreed that Henry Gosse should be approached. It was another example of the valuable support of his cousin, this time backing fully the recommendation of another. Henry was characteristically unsure about the project but produced two volumes for which SPCK paid £170.

Research for the SPCK volumes involved frequent visits to the Natural History section of the British Museum (the Natural History Museum in South Kensington was not opened until 1881) and these resulted in many contacts with other visitors. Being occupied on the volumes made Henry less self-absorbed and he was almost sociable at this time, with many of the contacts he made developing into important friendships. To improve access to the Museum, he moved to Kentish Town with his mother, and his elderly father joined them there.

During one of Henry's visits to the Museum, Josiah Whimper (or Whymper) suggested to him that he should write a book on oceans, as there was increasing interest in the sea during Victorian times and a fascination with all aspects of life in water. Henry subsequently approached the SPCK with the idea and they agreed to publish the book, paying Henry £120 for the copyright, and it appeared early in 1845, illustrated both by Gosse and Whimper. *The Ocean* [10] became as popular as was hoped and the descriptive text, combined with the illustrations of intriguing creatures and of exotic locations and events, resulted in such a demand that the book ran to many editions. It fitted well with the sense of adventure and exploration that was such a feature of the nineteenth century. With the publication of *The Ocean*, the disadvantage of signing away copyright became apparent to Henry and, as Freeman and Wertheimer point out in *Philip Henry*

Gosse: A Bibliography, he then decided to publish volumes while retaining copyright. Care with money was a characteristic of the man and no wonder after his earlier experiences and with his memory of the loss of his grandfather's wealth.

The popularity of Gosse's work increased while Henry was away in Jamaica. At a meeting at the British Museum, Edward Doubleday had suggested that Henry should collect insects in the tropics and he recommended Jamaica as a destination. The idea appealed to Henry and he made an agreement that the collection would be bought by Hugh Cuming of 80 Gower Street, London, and this would help to finance the visit. In addition to collecting insects, it was also a chance to look at all the Natural History of the island, little of which was known.

The family now left Kentish Town and Thomas and Hannah moved to a little house in Hackney. Once they were settled, Henry set sail for Jamaica on the *Caroline* on 20 October 1844, staying on the island for eighteen months in a large house called Bluefields. Very early in the visit Henry heard of the death of his father (he died as Henry was crossing the Atlantic), but this doesn't seem to have affected him too adversely. Bluefields was a good centre for Henry's collecting and observation of Natural History (but what site wouldn't be in unexplored Jamaica?) and he sent back a first batch of material with the returning *Caroline*. One of the most important people Henry met in Jamaica was a planter and local magistrate called Richard Hill who shot birds to preserve their skins, a habit that Henry had already acquired. The two enjoyed each other's company on many occasions during the visit and Henry had a high regard for Hill as a Natural Historian, so they collaborated. The stay in Jamaica ended on 26 June 1846 and Henry's journal of this exciting time was published in 1851 as *A Naturalist's Sojourn in Jamaica*, recognising Hill 'as a man of science, as a gentleman, and as a Christian'.

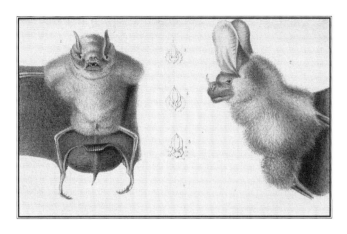

Illustration from *A Naturalist's Sojourn in Jamaica*.
(Reproduced with the permission of the Zoological Society of London).

On return from Jamaica, Henry had no steady income, so it was suggested to him by friends that he make another collecting trip, this time to the Azores. Some preliminary plans were in place, but were not put into effect because he finally began to receive income from his writing, from books published both by Van Voorst and the SPCK. *The Birds of Jamaica* 'was received with great respect by the world of science', and Henry acknowledged the influence and knowledge of his Jamaican friend Richard Hill on the title page 'greatly against that modest gentleman's wish'. There were always generous thanks from Henry to colleagues when these were due.

At about this time, Henry's commonest psychosomatic illness turned from headaches to dyspepsia and he suffered with this complaint for many years. His personality now fully formed, he retained his shyness and could appear austere and even severe when in conversation. Yet, there was little problem in making connections with fellow Natural Historians through visits to the British Museum. His was not an easy social manner and, of course, he was aware of that, but he was unaware that his psychosomatic illnesses had their origin in his personal conflicts.

The development of Henry Gosse's religious beliefs

Henry's father Thomas was a lover of poetry and he had a gentle, romantic nature, lacking drive and ambition. He was seemingly content to paint, write and travel to seek commissions but he was a Christian and the Gosse household was religious. This was not an age where secular views were common. It was the dour, ever-present Hannah who instilled strong Christian values in Henry and it is typical of her that she told him to read his Bible every day when he set sail for Newfoundland. The colony was dominated by Catholics, often of Irish descent, and this concerned Henry, especially as there was a call for independence and, no doubt, much near-riotous behaviour from the boisterous residents. From boyhood, Henry had a strong antipathy towards Catholics and this is a long-held tradition among Protestants, as Baptists had the same view in the 1950s and probably still do now. My childhood opinion that Catholics were wrong wasn't helped by their absence from the religious part of School Assemblies, together with Jewish pupils. Somehow, the two were grouped as non-believers in the true way to salvation and viewed as enemies. I was never able to understand why I should feel this way, but it was the received wisdom and I went along with it. Henry's feeling against Catholics from his early upbringing was certainly reinforced by events in Newfoundland, and his view that not all Christians were equal was hardened during his time there.

Henry was a member of the Wesleyan Society at the time he visited Newfoundland and, although his beliefs were not as intense as they were to become, they were certainly important to him. A quotation from the time of his sister Elizabeth's illness in 1832 shows this:

56

My prominent thought in this crisis was legal. I wanted the Almighty to be my Friend; to go to Him in my need. I knew He required me to be holy. He had said, "My son, give Me thy heart". I closed with him, not hypocritically, but sincerely; intending henceforth to live a new, a holy life; to lease and serve God. I knew nothing of my own weakness, or of the power of sin. I cannot say that I was born again as yet; but a work was commenced which was preparatory to, and which culminated in, regeneration.

Henry was on his way to a strong Christian belief and, typically for those that undergo this process, he began to feel that he could only mix freely with those of a similar religious persuasion. Mr and Mrs Jaques, Henry's friends in Newfoundland and Canada, were members of the same Wesleyan community and this drew Henry to them. The couple were undoubtedly a strong influence on him, and their common religious beliefs were a powerful factor behind their move to the farm together, for that enterprise was certainly based on faith in something rather than on a rational decision. Henry writes:

My friendship with the Jaqueses was very helpful to my spiritual life. It alienated me more and more from the companionship of the unconverted young men of the place; it was a marked commencement of that decided separateness from the world, which I have sought to maintain ever since.

His 'separateness from the world' was to put him beyond any consideration of views that hinted at opposition to the literal truth of the Bible. As Edmund Gosse wrote in *The Naturalist of the Sea-Shore: The Life of Philip Henry Gosse*:

...his code was the Bible, and the Bible only, without any modern modification whatever; without allowance for any difference between the old world and the new, without any distinction of value in parts, without the smallest concession to the critical spirit upon any point; and absolute, uncompromising, unquestioning reliance on the Hebrew and Greek texts as inspired by the mouth of God and uncorrupted by the hand of man. [9]

Henry's profound Christian beliefs burst through frequently in his wonderful writing about plants and animals, and he was compelled to proselytise. Whether this was to convince others, or to reassure himself, is a moot point. It was not only in his writing that Henry spread the Message. Although shy, he spoke to people he met about their need for salvation and an early example of this practice came during the voyage back to England from Alabama on the *Isaac Newton*. No doubt, his fellow passengers viewed Henry in a guarded way after his enquiries and, as a sensitive man, he must have been aware of their reaction to his approach.

When he moved to Hackney, Henry's religious views were influenced by the writings of Matthew Habershon, whose sons happened to be at his school. Looking back on 1842, a crux year in his religious thinking, Henry wrote:

> Of the Restoration of the Jews, I had received some dim inkling already,....; but of the destruction of the papacy, the end of Gentilism, the kingdom of God, the resurrection and rapture of the Church at the personal descent of the Lord, and the imminency of this, – all came on me that evening like a flash of lightning.

A flash of lightning describes well the force of this revelation. The Second Coming, and its imminence, was thereafter the most important factor in shaping Henry's approach to life. However, there was no prediction of the date when Christ would return, so believers had to be constantly watchful and ready.

In Hackney, Henry became friendly with William and Mary Berger who were members of the Brethren. They met for worship and for scripture study, and the group believed strongly that they needed to be separate from the rest of the World, an approach which Henry had decided upon after his time with Mr and Mrs Jaques. His isolation from differing views was now complete and it stayed with him for the rest of his life as the Brethren confirmed, and strengthened, his narrow standpoint. Once settled in St Marychurch in 1857, Henry led his own group called 'The Church of Christ in this Parish', to whom he preached. It is likely that his fellow worshippers looked up to him as he was well known and one can imagine that this response tightened even more firmly his adherence to an immovable belief.

Henry's convictions for much of his life were thus unchanging and invulnerable and, while enjoying argument, he never shifted his beliefs. He was a profound literalist and one with a great knowledge of the Biblical text, its exegesis and nuances. Yet, Henry had contacts in the world of Natural History and these were based on the mutual respect in knowledge of plants and animals. He corresponded with many colleagues in this way, but a little Christian proselytising could creep in occasionally, just as it did, in fuller measure, in some of his books.

Aside from his contacts among Natural Historians, Edmund remarked that his father did not have friends but 'strong acquaintanceships', who were put off by the 'unyielding surface of his conscience'. Yet, throughout his early life Henry made strong friendships where interests were shared, so this lack of close friendship came after the conversion to his own brand of religion. His letters to members of the family were said to be full of long words and different in style to the lightness of touch shown in much of his finest writing on Natural History.

The image created by Edmund is of a dour and unyielding man, perhaps a little like my own grandfather. Nevertheless, we know from his books that he could be cheerful and enthusiastic and this stemmed from a child-like appreciation of the natural world around him.

Henry Gosse's own family

Henry's first-recorded, serious romantic involvement came when he met a girl called Amelia Button in Wimborne when he was nearly 30 years old. We have his less than flattering description of Amelia as 'an accomplished, pious and winning lady, older than I, and much pitted with the small-pox', with whom he formed a 'very tender attachment.' This shows Henry's honesty when describing people and their appearance; the same approach used to describe plants and animals. There is no room for nicety and one hopes that Henry's private conversations with Amelia were a little less blunt. We can only guess at his courting style, but it was most likely formal, awkward and lacking in confidence. Unfortunately, Henry had no money or prospects and Amelia instead became engaged to a Wesleyan minister, leaving him rather hurt by the experience. On moving to London, where his only close contact was his cousin Thomas Bell, Henry must have endured a bleak period emotionally, although this was relieved by the acceptance of *The Canadian Naturalist* by Van Voorst. This breakthrough not only opened the way for Henry to become a professional writer; it was also likely to increase his prospects as a potential husband.

Inevitably, Henry found his future wife at a church meeting, as a similar Christian standpoint was essential for a successful match. Emily Bowes, an American whose father had been shipped out of Boston after the Tea Party, attended the Brethren meetings in Hackney and it was there that she and Henry met. When he came to England, Emily's father was wealthy, but Mr Bowes had since given most of his money away. Hearing of this from Emily must have created an empathetic response, as Henry's grandfather had also lost a fortune.

Emily was born in England on 10 November 1806 and was thus older than Henry, just as Amelia had been nearly ten years before. She worked as a governess, having received a good education, and she and Henry shared a love of poetry as well as having similar religious interests. Henry must also have spoken many times of his experiences in North America and this was yet another area of common ground. Although not disfigured, as poor Amelia had been, Emily had freckles which were considered unattractive at the time. She looked young for her age and had a lively personality and it is easy to see that the buttoned-up Henry was captured by her vivacity and, somehow overcoming his inhibitions, he proposed to Emily 'quite abruptly, and without premeditation' on 17 September 1848. They were married two months later, when Emily was 42 and Henry 38.

Before marriage, Emily had enjoyed an active social life with a circle of women friends, but Henry did not welcome visitors, stemming partly from his shyness and partly because he didn't want to be disturbed in his research and writing. Now that he was receiving income from his books, the couple moved to a larger property in de Beauvoir Square, Hackney, where Emily spent a lot of time in his study (she was the only person other than Henry who was allowed to enter), working silently on annotating a Bible. As Edmund remarked on this change in her way of life, '... the strain was very real, the sudden cloistered seclusion from the open world very trying and distressing.'

Henry, meanwhile, had developed his fascination for microscopy and, especially with the biology of rotifers. His correspondence with the leading microscopists of the time brought appreciation for his work by the scientific community and, quite characteristically, he became absorbed to the apparent exclusion of other events. His artificial ponds in the garden, used for keeping rotifers, were looked upon with some fear by neighbours as cholera was prevalent at that time, but that was not likely to distract someone of Henry's character. His first paper on rotifers was published in 1850 and as detailed in the Bibliography by Freeman and Wertheimer he produced seventeen papers in total on these organisms. A comprehensive work on rotifers already existed, published by Ehrenberg in German, and Emily, who knew the language, was able to translate for Henry. Apparently, he awaited each section of new material with 'feverish anxiety.' Eventually, a book and supplement, co-authored by Hudson and Gosse and based on their joint researches, were published much later in 1886 and 1889. It is regarded as a classic of its type.

Although engaged with the study of rotifers, Henry faced a significant change when he became a father. Edmund cites an oft-quoted entry in Henry's diary that read: 'E. delivered of a son. Received green swallow from Jamaica.' Edmund was born on 21 September 1849 when Henry was 39 and Emily nearly 43 and the diary entry arguably fuelled the son's feeling of distance from the father when he read it as an adult. As in all things, the birth was something to report along with other biological events and Edmund probably makes too much of the brevity of the entry. Henry must have been elated, although there would now be a marked alteration of his domestic routine and he knew it.

Henry was planning to return to the West Indies in November 1850, accompanied by Emily. However, she became ill and he decided against making the trip. We don't know how much discussion occurred between the couple on the subject, but it was probably very little, Emily receiving the news in a letter 'worded in terms of the most devoted affection.' It makes one wonder how they communicated affection at all in conversation. Edmund describes Henry up to this time as leading a life which was 'cloistered and uniform in the extreme' but his increasing reputation as a scientist, aquarist and popular author on Natural History meant that he received many social invitations. He turned them all down on the basis that he did not have the time – a typical excuse of the socially inhibited. He also strongly disliked what we now call small talk.

The lack of outside activities must surely have made Emily's life seem even more secluded, although she now had the distraction of Edmund. Henry maintained contacts with a few scientific acquaintances and went to meetings of various societies and they both went to meetings of the Brethren. This confined life, and the need to publish to earn money and perhaps the strain of being a new father, brought on a further bout of psychosomatic illness. By now, Hannah Gosse, their acting housekeeper, had moved to separate lodgings and Henry and Emily both took to their beds. It was decided that they needed a change of surroundings, so they set off for South Devon in January 1852.

This was the period when Henry began to refine his aquaria and he spent much time collecting from the shore around Torquay and travelling to other places in the south west. It was exhilarating and led to *A Naturalist's Rambles on the Devonshire Coast*. Although their accommodation in St Marychurch provided a good centre for all these activities, Henry again began to suffer headaches and the family moved to spend time in North Devon. Whether because of the change of air, or the distraction of new collecting areas, Henry felt much better, although both he and Emily fell ill again after the summer. They decided to spend the winter in London, where Henry made contact with Warington to work on aquaria, and the family then moved to Weymouth in the spring, allowing further collection and observation of plants and animals. There were further episodes of psychosomatic illness, and the dispute with the Zoological Society added to the stress of overwork, but visits were made to sites in southern England and south Wales. Emily occupied herself writing religious tracts, so she had an outlet both for her creative side and her need to proselytise. She wrote forty-one of these tracts and their circulation extended to hundreds of thousands worldwide, bringing Emily fame in the limited circle that meant so much to her. I wonder if any of the tracts from the Evangelical Tract Society, which I hoarded at Torquay Boys' Grammar School, had been written by Emily?

Philip Henry Gosse aged 45.
(With permission of the National Portrait Gallery).

With one or two exceptions, this continued to be a very happy time for Henry and, increasingly, for Emily. By 1856 Edmund records:

Under her care, all that was warmest and brightest in Philip Gosse's character had been developed; he had ceased to shun his kind; he had lost his shyness, and had become one of the most genial, if still one of the most sententious of men.

What a contrast. He knew he was loved, was pleased with the recognition he was accorded, was receiving an income and was able to do what he enjoyed most: to worship God and study Natural History. This marvellous phase was not to last sadly, and the family was shortly to undergo a terrible and traumatic time when Emily became very seriously ill. Edmund writes of this and the dramatic change that it brought: ' ... now the gloom was to close again over their life, and they were to pass together, through anguish of body and mind, into the valley of the shadow of death.' The difference in the mood of these two quotes reveals the devastating change brought by Emily's condition. In late April, she had soreness in her left breast and was persuaded to consult a local physician, Dr Edward Laseron, who diagnosed cancer, informing Emily in a candid and direct manner. Even though this must have been frightening and a terrible shock, Emily returned home and only told Henry some hours later. The following day they wisely consulted Dr Henry Salter (a distant relative of Henry's, being a grandson of Aunt Bell), who recommended that they also consult with Sir James Paget, the leading authority on cancer at the time, who unfortunately confirmed the diagnosis and recommended immediate surgery. Emily did not want to go through with it as she hated pain, and anaesthetics were not used at this time. As an alternative, Salter recommended consulting Jesse Weldon Fell, an American residing in Pimlico, who used a 'secret medicament' as a means of curing cancer without surgery. This 'purple mucilaginous substance' was derived from the rhizome of *Sanguinaria canadensis*, a member of the poppy family, and was known as 'puccoon' among Cherokee Indians, who used it in many herbal cures. Emily's treatment with this substance is described in detail in a paper by L. R. Croft, [11] and, although it was far from painless, both she and Henry remained optimistic.

As a diversion, Henry kept busy and went collecting off Deal and also completed arrangements for a Natural History field course at Tenby. Fell had given approval for Emily to travel to Wales, so they were able to visit Tenby together. She was provided with a supply of medication and the confidence of the physician led Emily and Henry to think at this time that the likelihood of death from the cancer was remote. However, Emily's condition worsened during the visit to Tenby and she sat on the sands and chatted to people passing by, something which she found easy and in which she had a gift. The pain of her illness enhanced her ability to empathise with those who had problems, but she was now seriously ill and both Emily and Henry were concerned at her condition and the effect of travelling back to London. They were able to return in early October and Fell recommended more severe treatments, which required Emily and 7-year-old Edmund to move near to his practice. They took uncomfortable lodgings in Pimlico and Henry joined them at week-ends, Emily and Edmund being alone for the rest of the time. Given Emily's condition, it must have been a comfort to have the boy with her, but also a dreadful strain. For Edmund, it must have been most difficult and bewildering as he was so young. It is easy to see how his father's absence during these trying days and nights would cause resentment and Edmund writes about this phase with clear feelings of desperation. Henry was removing himself from watching Emily's suffering but what was he to do? As a 'runner' myself, I can see an argument for being most useful in short bursts of support, although this is not an excuse for leaving Edmund in the way that he did.

Emily's condition grew worse and the very painful extra treatments provided no relief, only more agony. She used opiates to control the pain and now Fell declared her case hopeless. On 24 December, she was treated by Dr John Epps a homeopathic physician, but this, of course, was of no value other than in providing the hope of a placebo effect. Henry and Emily now had to face the imminent reality of her death. A cousin, Mrs Morgan, came voluntarily to nurse and support them both, and this kindness was appreciated greatly by the family. Emily died in the early hours of 10 February 1857 and she was buried in Abney Park cemetery, which was favoured by missionaries and other religious figures.

In coping with bereavement, Henry was sustained by his faith and didn't show outward signs of grief, although he was deeply affected. It was a severe blow and Edmund comments that Henry never regained his full energy afterwards. Emily's support, cheerfulness and ability to take in new ideas, so important in drawing Henry out, were no longer there. To overcome his suppressed grief he wrote *A Memorial of the Last Days on Earth of Emily Gosse* [12] in which he detailed her illness with typical candour. Henry's description in the *Memorial* of her last weeks was described by Edmund as 'self-torturing', but it was his way of admitting that this tragedy had occurred. It was only intended for a small and limited circle of readers, including Emily's friends, but they were upset by the cold description (I should add that I have not read the book, so my information on this is second-hand – for some reasons linked to my own family experiences, I couldn't face reading it). Typically, the response to the *Memorial* surprised Henry, for whom accurate description was everything and who was not sufficiently aware that this may cause emotional distress in others. While writing it may have been cathartic for him, the response to the *Memorial* sent Henry back to his old ways and he became locked in again, just as he had been before his marriage.

The household was now settled in St Marychurch, Torquay where they moved shortly after Emily's death. Although far from the target of holidaymakers that I remember, Torbay and the English Riviera were becoming discovered by genteel Victorians and there was much new building. The South Devon Railway had completed their line to a station in Torquay (now named Torre) in 1849 and this allowed uninterrupted travel from London and other parts of the country. The Dartmouth and Torbay Railway was founded to continue the line on to Torquay seafront and thence to Paignton and Kingswear, an extension completed in 1864 and which greatly influenced my summer Saturdays as a boy. This extension was therefore made after Henry's move to live permanently in St. Marychurch, and he would have been very aware of its construction so close to the sea. Henry and Edmund were among the first wave of Victorian settlers at a time when large houses and villas were being built and Henry bought a new house that was yet to be completed. He moved there with Edmund in September 1857 and the house was given the name Sandhurst. It was where he later constructed the re-circulating aquarium system. The house still stands and I have visited it, although there have been many extensions and alterations since Henry's time.

Hannah Gosse came to live with her son and grandson in March 1858 until her death on 28 February 1860, aged 80. Henry continued to collect and observe aquatic life enthusiastically and a dramatic change in circumstances occurred in the autumn and early winter of 1860. Henry became friendly with a visitor to Torquay, Miss Eliza Brightwen, who was four years his junior. The friendship blossomed, with Henry both flattered and seemingly infatuated by Eliza's attention. It certainly resulted in a less sombre home life for Edmund. After a rapid courtship, Henry proposed to Eliza and they were married in Frome on 18 December 1860, when Henry was 50 and Eliza 46. We do not know how Henry reconciled the idea of being re-united with his two wives in Heaven.

By January 1865, Henry 'ceased to be a professional writer' and the remainder of his life was spent in retirement in St Marychurch. He was happier and more content than he had been and his health was good or, rather, he had less psychosomatic aches and pains. He continued to make marine collecting trips and, on 19 September 1887, was visiting Goodrington Sands with Eliza, Edmund, Edmund's wife and three children and was full of his usual enthusiasms. It was one of the areas of Torbay where I used to spend a lot of time as a boy, so I can easily imagine the young members of the family running around and listening to Henry as he described creatures he turned up from the rock pools. Edmund and family were forerunners of the large numbers of holidaymakers who flocked to Paignton when I was young, although these visitors didn't have an expert on hand to answer questions about marine plants and animals, as Edmund's children did. Henry wrote to the Edmund Gosses staying in Paignton the day after the Goodrington visit, with thanks for such a happy day. The relationship between father and son was intact, despite the difficulties between them, and there was always close contact between Henry and his grandchildren when they met during visits.

Goodrington Sands East. (From Author's Collection).

Henry Gosse as a teacher, lecturer and scientist

In addition to his legacy of published works in Natural History, Henry will also have been recalled by contemporaries as a lecturer and we know that Henry was an innovative teacher. In Hackney he had made the boys draw plans of the school and of the residences along the road before looking at maps from the wider World. It was to give them a sense of scale and an insight into how maps are produced. He also took them on insect collecting trips to Epping Forest, showing them both his knowledge and his great enthusiasm. With the publication of *A Naturalist's Rambles on the Devonshire Coast* in 1853 and *The Aquarium: an unveiling of the wonders of the deep sea* in 1854, Henry was recognised as a notable figure in the world of Natural History and he received invitations to lecture and did so throughout England and Scotland. Although he had preached many times, Henry had no experience of lecturing and had to develop his own style, described as being 'serene and dignified.' His preaching meant he had overcome a fear of public speaking and he was a popular lecturer, Edmund believing that his father could have been an excellent orator as he had a 'scrupulous elegance of language' while preaching, and was expressive when reading poetry aloud to small groups and to the family. His lectures were illustrated by free drawings on the blackboard and Henry's talent as an artist would have been impressive in itself.

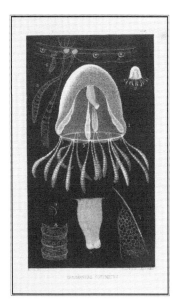 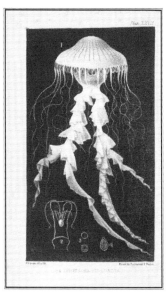

(Left) *Traumantias corynetes*; (Right) *Chrysaora cyclonota*.
From *A Naturalist's Rambles on the Devonshire Coast*.

In addition to his lectures, Henry also led field courses for groups of amateurs interested in learning more about marine life and the first formal course was held in Ilfracombe in the summer of 1855. It was advertised by means of circulars and also by word of mouth from Charles Kingsley who had become a friend and admirer of Henry's. They enjoyed a regular correspondence, both having lived in Torquay, and Kingsley suggested that Clovelly in North Devon would be a good place to collect, although it is not known if the group ventured that far from Ilfracombe. The course entailed several hours of collecting material from shores, followed by observation and identification work indoors. Whilst we cannot be sure how this, and subsequent courses, were received, it is probable that Henry's enthusiasm for marine plants and animals conveyed itself to those attending and they must have been impressed by his knowledge and authority in making identifications.

There were also informal contacts on the shore. Edmund describes a later, casual encounter when collecting with his father at on the rocky coast at Livermead in Torbay – the same spot where I was later to make collections.

Rocks at Livermead. (From Author's Collection).

Although usually wary and put off by fellow collectors, Henry overheard a group of women discussing a rarity that they had found. Despite his rather eccentric appearance, featuring thigh-length rubber boots and an elderly felt hat discoloured by age and salt, he approached the group and informed them that their rarity had been mis-identified and was indeed of a common species. It seems that the women were not put off by Henry's intrusion and maintained that it was a rarity, citing a work by P. H. Gosse as their authority! We don't know the resolution of this little conflict but surely true to character Henry would have corrected them, but with civility and, hopefully, with humour. All records suggest that Henry was at his most relaxed when out collecting.

Another chance meeting between Henry and a fellow enthusiast came when the Gosse family made their visit to Tenby for two months during 1854. One day, Henry was approached by a gentleman who introduced himself as Bishop Samuel Wilberforce of Oxford, later to feature large in the famous 1860 debate on evolution with T. H. Huxley. Henry and the bishop corresponded on a few occasions after this meeting, although it was not a close contact and must have brought some discomfort for Henry, as Wilberforce was a High Churchman and thus almost a Catholic in Henry's eyes. 1856 saw the return of the Gosse family to Tenby where Henry had agreed to preach and to conduct a further field course, the format being the same as the one in Ilfracombe held the year before, with collection followed by talks and identification sessions. It was during this visit to Tenby that Emily's condition became noticeably worse and she couldn't take part in collecting.

At the time Henry was becoming well known to the general public as a Natural Historian, his work in Zoology was being recognised by the scientific community. A full listing of his publications in scientific journals is given by Freeman and Wertheimer in their Bibliography; Henry's first paper was a list of the butterflies of Lower Canada published in the *Entomologist* in 1841. Some of these butterflies may very well have been residents of the insect cabinet that just survived transport on Mr Jaques' wagon. In the rest of the 1840s, Henry had papers in the *Zoologist* and in the *Annals and Magazine of Natural History*, mainly on insects, and he continued to publish in both these journals during the 1850s, when papers also appeared in the *Transactions of the Microscopical Society*, the *Quarterly Journal of Microscopical Science*, the *Philosophical Transactions of the Royal Society*, and the *Transactions of the Linnean Society of London*. Despite his lack of formal training, he was now an established figure in mainstream science and, from 1846 to 1856, thirty-one papers were published, with lizards, rotifers and sea anemones being common subjects. A further fourteen papers were published in 1857 to 1858, mainly on rotifers, sea anemones and corals, but with one on moths; nineteen papers appeared from 1859 to 1863, and three in 1865, when there was a shift away from terrestrial and aquatic animals to orchids, which had become Henry's new passion. He published no further papers until 1877 (it was the time of his 'happy retirement') and his last papers, published in 1883 and 1887, gave symmetry to his list of publications as their subjects were butterflies and rotifers.

It is interesting that papers by Gosse are still used by the scientific community and his record of citations (something that is important in assigning status in the contemporary scientific world) compares well with that of his cousin Thomas Bell FRS (1792-1880), William Pengelly FRS (1812-1894) (Torquay's 'other' FRS, an expert on cave faunas, and a contemporary of Henry Gosse), and that of his supporter Sir Ray Lankester FRS (1847-1929), (Professor of Zoology and Comparative Anatomy at UCL, 1874-1891). The latter was described by Harte and North in *The World of University College London 1828-1978* as: 'a dominating figure in his subject, editing the major zoological journal of the period for fifty years and placing his pupils in many of the chairs in the subject at home and in the Empire.' [13] A comparison from the Web of Science[SM] database shows the following statistics for the number of citations made in papers published since 1946 (the first year of entries for Henry Gosse in the database) for these four eminent men:

	Number of citations since 1946	Number of citations in last 20 years	Number of citations in last 10 years
GOSSE	332	155	98
BELL	286	191	130
PENGELLY	33	18	15
LANKESTER	100	29	18

On that basis, Henry Gosse compares well and his scientific work is shown to have lasting importance.

In addition to the papers there were books of scholarship to go alongside his more popular writings on Natural History and those designed for education. The books were illustrated, or part-illustrated, by Henry and those who have seen well-preserved originals describe their beauty and fine colouration. I have been fortunate to see several First Editions of Henry's books and can vouch for these qualities. He was a first class biological illustrator. Of the larger works, *The Birds of Jamaica* was published in 1847; *Actinologia Britannica. A history of the British sea-anemones and corals. With coloured figures of the species and principal varieties* in 1860, and *The Rotifera; or wheel animalcules. With illustrations. In two volumes*, (authored by C. T. Hudson, assisted by P. H. Gosse) in 1886, the latter benefitting from Emily Gosse's translations of German texts.

Illustrations from *Actinologia Britannica.*

In addition to publishing books and articles in journals, Henry attended meetings of the learned societies of the time, many of which still meet today. After he had presented a paper on rotifers at The Royal Society in March 1856, it was proposed that Henry be made a Fellow and this honour was bestowed in June of that year. Becoming an FRS brought Henry and Emily much pleasure, the more so as he had not had the university training obtained by many professional scientists of the time. Tragically, this enjoyment was to be short-lived as Emily's illness now dominated their lives. During this difficult time, Henry continued his correspondence with fellow Zoologists and Edmund cites several letters written between Henry and Charles Darwin, who was finalising the synthesis of the ideas that led to *On the Origin of Species*, published in 1859. Henry replied to all Darwin's correspondence: on variation in pigeons; transport of plants and animals to distant islands; larval molluscs adhering to duck's feet, and the effects of transmission on the feet of birds – 'with ample notes.' Henry was also approached at this time to be the first holder of a Chair in Natural History in a new university institution that was proposed for the grounds of Gnoll Park near Neath in South Wales. This idea excited him, but the scheme came to nothing and Henry was left disappointed as he knew that he was good at teaching and lecturing.

Henry's contact with the Scientific Establishment changed dramatically with Emily's tragic illness and death. Without her support, he no longer went to meetings of the Learned Societies and, even if he did, he would be unlikely to enjoy what was being discussed. Whether it was because of the loss of Emily and her guiding hand, his awareness of developing thinking towards evolution, or some other motivation, Henry now published his most controversial work, *Omphalos*.

1 Gosse, P. H., *A Naturalist's Rambles on the Devonshire Coast*, (John Van Voorst), London, 1853.

2 Brock, W. H., The Warington-Gosse aquarium controversy: two unrecorded letters, *Archives of Natural History*, 18, 1991, pp. 179-183.

3 Gosse, P. H., *The Aquarium: an unveiling of the wonders of the deep sea*, (John Van Voorst), London, 1854.

4 Gosse, P. H., *A Handbook to the Marine Aquarium*, (John Van Voorst), London, 1855.

5 Freeman, R. B., and Wertheimer, D, *Philip Henry Gosse: A Bibliography*, (Dawson Publishing), Folkestone, 1980.

6 Thwaite, A. *Edmund Gosse; A Literary Landscape*, (Tempus Publishing), Stroud, 2007.

7 Gosse, P. H. *Evenings at the Microscope; or researches among the minuter forms of animal life*, (Society for Promoting Christian Knowledge), London, 1859.

8 Hand, C, and Hendrickson, J. R., 'A two- tentacled, commensal hydroid from California', (Limnomedusae, Proboscidactyla), *Biological Bulletin*, 99, 1950, pp. 74-87.

9 Gosse, E, *The Naturalist of the Sea-Shore; The Life of Philip Henry Gosse*, (K. Paul Trench, Trütner & Co. Ltd.), London, 1890.

10 Gosse, P. H., *The Ocean*, (SPCK), London, 1845.

11 Croft, L. R., 'Edmund Gosse and the "New and Fantastic Cure" for Breast Cancer', *Medical History*, 38, (1994), pp. 143–159.

12 Gosse, P. H., *A Memorial of the Last Days on Earth of Emily Gosse*, (James Nisbet), London, 1857.

13 Harte, N, and North, J., *The World of University College London 1828-1978*, (Eyre and Spottiswode), London, 1979.

Omphalos and
The Romance of
Natural History

Untying the Geological Knot

And God said, Let the earth bring forth grass, the herb yielding seed, and the fruit tree yielding fruit after his kind, whose seed is in itself, upon the earth: and it was so. And God said, Let the waters bring forth abundantly the moving creature that hath life, and fowl that may fly above the earth in the open firmament of heaven. And God created great whales, and every living creature that moveth, which the waters brought forth abundantly, after their kind, and every winged fowl after his kind: and God saw that it was good. And God blessed them, saying, Be fruitful, and multiply, and fill the waters in the seas, and let fowl multiply in the earth. And God said, Let the earth bring forth the living creature after his kind, cattle, and creeping thing, and beast of the earth after his kind: and it was so. And God saw every thing that he had made, and, behold, it was very good. And the evening and the morning were the sixth day.

Selected verses from Genesis 1, *King James' Bible.*

*O*mphalos was published in November 1857, just weeks after Henry's and Edmund's arrival to live in St Marychurch. Henry must have been working on the text during Emily's illness, and then after her death in February of that year and it is probable that it was written alongside *A memorial of the Last Days on Earth of Emily Gosse* [1] which was on sale in the summer of 1857.

The bereavement left a deep sadness, whatever Henry's beliefs about the afterlife and it was a time when he needed his profound faith in The Bible, just when the Biblical account of Creation was being challenged in some scientific circles. Henry knew, both from reading, and from attending scientific meetings that the concept of geological time was becoming accepted widely, and he needed to set out his view of the Creation, based on the literal truth of The Bible. The full title of the book is *Omphalos: an attempt to untie the geological knot* [2] and Henry felt that he could reconcile the differences between science and religion, and provide an explanation of how events apparently taking place over geological time did not challenge his biblical view that the Earth is only a few thousand years old. It was Henry at his most personal, all driven by a difficult time in his life, both emotionally and as a Natural Historian and scientist. *Omphalos* is written in two parts and is set as a trial: 'A High Court of Inquiry' to use Henry's phrase. It begins with the case for geological time and this is followed by a lengthy cross-examination of the evidence.

First to appear is 'The Witness for the Macro-Chronology' (or geological time scales) who is not living and 'his testimony, therefore is not oral, but written – lithographed, in fact.' Henry's oblique reference to geology thus sets the tone for the book. It begins with an introduction to the evidence presented by these rock strata, with igneous granite forming the base. Subsequent contractions of cooling rock resulted in fractures and dislocations, and broken rock was fragmented further and carried by water to be deposited as layers on top of the granite. Henry, on behalf of The Witness for the Macro-Chronology, argues that it must have taken a long time for these processes to occur:

> The deposition of these strata, being formed out of granite, supposes the pre-existence of that rock; and as they occur in vast thicknesses, even of many thousand feet, then separation, deposition, and re-

consolidation must have occupied, however rapidly we may suppose the processes to have been accomplished, considerable periods of time.

Next, there is a description of the wide range of fossils recognised from the 'numerous strata that overlie the rocks of granitic origin.' Henry declares that these were distinct from their modern relatives and, as their remains were deposited in deep strata, it is fair to assume that he also knew that they must have existed for a considerable time. Throughout the evidence, the accepted names for geological time periods are used, so that there is no confusion of terms with those used in science at the time.

We learn that great changes occurred within the Carboniferous where there were large deposits of coralline limestone in shallow seas, while plant remains were compressed into coal in swamps on land and on marine coasts. Henry is well aware of the quantity of vegetable material needed to produce these coal seams and 'nothing ... is more certain than that all coal was once vegetable; for in most cases woody structure may be detected under the microscope.' There is also no questioning of the length of time needed to create coal, with Henry quoting from McCulloch's *System of Geology* in describing just one major coal seam as likely to have taken 600,000 years to have been formed. He continues by describing the appearance of the first reptiles during this period, alluding also to the description of fossil footprints from very large reptiles which had been discovered in the roof of a coal mine.

Having discussed rock strata, in the next chapter he describes evidence that large-scale changes in stratification occurred over time. This was nearly fifty years before ideas on continental drift came to the fore and a hundred years before the acceptance of plate tectonics, so these play no part in the account. Henry describes the effect of the molten core on the Earth's crust, erupting through volcanoes to create magma intrusions and he relates how large earthquakes resulted in the fracture, and change in inclination, of strata. Such events occurred until the Old Red Sandstones were deposited and then, during a quiet phase until after the Carboniferous, there was a further time of great change in geological structure:

The effects of these convulsions were manifest in the changed relations of land and sea, existing continents and islands being dislocated, severed, and swallowed up, while others were elevated from the depths of the previous ocean.

Deposits that had been washed out by wave action led to New Red Sandstones and, although these may contain organic matter, Henry points to a gap in the fossil record between the remains of organisms that had been seen up until this time and those which were to follow. However, there were tracks:

The most interesting traces of the earth's tenants during the New Red formation consist of foot-tracks impressed by the progress of animals along the yielding mud between ranges of high and low tide. They afford a remarkable example (not, I think, sufficiently dwelt on) of the extreme rapidity with which deposits were consolidated; since the tracks must have been made, and the material consolidated, during the few hours, at most, that intervened between the recess and the reflux of the tide; since, if the mud had not so soon become solid, the flow of the sea would have instantly obliterated such marks, as it does now on our shores.

He goes on to detail other traces in the surface of the ancient mud of this period; trails, ripples, and even minute pits left by raindrops, the shape of the pits showing the direction of the driving rain that formed them. I find the idea of fossilised depressions of various kinds difficult to understand, but accept that they must have occurred and that unusual processes were involved in their preservation, when most were simply washed away. Henry, although quizzical, had no such problems in accepting their formation and he goes on to describe the fossil animals, especially terrestrial reptiles, found during the following Jurassic period. Among the profusion of other animals found were crinoids, ammonites, armed sharks and aquatic reptiles, all residents of the oceans.

Some reptile fossils contain materials within the gut, showing the last meal that the animals took before dying, and, if associated with the animals which produce it, fossilised faecal matter allows us to gain some further information on diets. We thus know about the structure of the animals and also something of their way of life. Several of the animals are illustrated in Henry's excellent woodcuts, which not only show their appearance but, in many cases, the habitat in which they were imagined to live. Henry's training in the art of the miniature certainly showed to good effect in these illustrations and there are 56 woodcuts of various subjects in *Omphalos*. They must have taken some time to produce, but Henry was quite used to that level of effort.

Labyrinthodon pachygnathus from *Omphalos*.

Plesiosaurus dolichodeirus and *P. macrocephalus* from *Omphalos.*

The changing land masses of this geological period also supported new types of plants and insects and Henry points out that Western Europe was, at this time, a group of islands. It was into the shallow seas around the islands that the bodies of organisms with calcareous coverings, or inclusions, began to accumulate to form chalk, with nodules in the chalk having their origins in the siliceous spicules or coverings of sponges, protozoans or diatoms. After this period of relative calm, there followed another phase of convulsive change, with shallow marine strata being uplifted and with more magma intrusions of molten rock seeping through fissures and cracks.

Henry, continuing to represent The Witness for the Macro-Chronology, then describes how the London Clays were laid down, containing seeds from plants we know to have a preference for hot climates. Animals began to appear that are closely related to the contemporary fauna. Many familiar fish were present in the oceans, although of different species to those we have today, with Henry stating: '... not a single member of the great

Salmon family was yet introduced.' Alongside the appearance of fish that we would recognise came the disappearance of the large reptiles, and the occurrence on land of birds and mammals. These times were characterised by the presence of pachyderms, but much smaller relatives of the elephants, rhinoceroses and hippopotamuses which are familiar today. There continued to be changes in sea level and also in the upward movement of mountain chains.

Moving to the middle Tertiary we see a whole new range of pachyderms, including some giants, which were probably aquatic and were allied to the manatees and dugongs. He describes the preservation of elephants and rhinoceroses in icy avalanches and adds that the climate of these regions was not tropical, as evidenced by the hair covering of the mammoth. Not only pachyderms had close relatives today. Henry quotes Lyell, who published data in 1841 showing the 'gradual but rapid approximation of the tertiary fauna to that of the present.' This is a curious statement for Henry to make, as it could be used by an evolutionist to describe changes in species through time.

Being a Victorian Englishman, Henry had thus far concentrated on Britain and the continent of Europe, as Great Britain was perceived to be the most important country on Earth. The Witness for the Macro-Chronology, now turns to other regions, describing animals such as the moa and the dodo, which were recently extinct. He concludes the evidence for changes over geological time with a summary, as would be the case in a court of law. This gives, point by point, the evidence presented, where Henry accepts that long time periods were required for all the changes we have seen in both rock strata and in the appearance of different plants and animals. Life forms appear and disappear rather than evolve, but, nonetheless, there is acceptance that all the changes took very much longer than in the literal Biblical account, which describes the Earth and all living things being created in six days, just thousands of years ago. Here, then, we have the irreconcilable conflict between the evidence which Henry presents as The Witness for the Macro-Chronology (with his usual skill and devotion to accuracy) and his religious beliefs. The purpose of *Omphalos* was to untie this geological knot and Henry attempts this in the rest of the book. He maintains the legalistic format by using cross-examination to defend his views against this apparently overwhelming evidence.

He begins by stating that more information could have been presented in the evidence for the macro-chronology, but he felt limited by space (even though this section comprised nearly one third of the book). He declares that he was '... not conscious of having in any degree cushioned, or concealed, or understated a single proof which would have helped the conclusion.' I agree, but now it is time for Henry to present his case. He begins by saying that the evidence presented by the Witness for the Macro-Chronology is circumstantial, as no-one witnessed any of the geological processes described, or saw alive the organisms which are present as fossils. Nevertheless, we can identify fossil bones and have very strong evidence that they came from a recognisable skeleton and that this was the remains of a creature that was once alive:

And then experience has shown that the skeleton is made in a particular manner. The bone is deposited, atom by atom, in living organic cells, which are formed by living blood, which implies a living animal. The microscopic texture of your stone-girt skeleton does not differ from that of the skeleton which you cleaned from the muscles with your own hands; and therefore you infer that it was constructed in the same way, namely, by the blood of a living body .... Well, I come back, notwithstanding, to my position, – that your right to affirm this must altogether depend on the exhaustive power of that experience on which you build. And it will be overthrown, if I can show that skeletons have been made in some other way than by the agency of living blood ... Can I do this? I think I can. At least I think I can show enough greatly to diminish, if not altogether to destroy, the confidence with which you inferred the existence of vast periods of past time from geological phenomena. I can adduce a principle, having the universality (within its proper sphere) of LAW, hitherto unrecognised, whose tendency is to invalidate the testimony of your witness.

Strong words, and now we wait for Henry to give his testimony and, through doing so, show what really happened when the Earth and living organisms appeared. He begins with two postulates:

1. The creation of matter: 'I assume that at some period or other in past eternity there existed nothing but the Eternal God, and that He called the universe into being out of nothing'; and

2. The persistence of species: 'I demand also, in opposition to the development hypothesis, the perpetuity of specific characters, from the moment when the respective creatures were called into being, till they cease to be. I assume that each organism which the Creator educed was stamped with an indelible specific character, which made it what it was, and distinguished it from everything else, however near or like.'

Just as our knowledge of continental drift and plate tectonics was long after Henry's time, so was the idea of the 'Big Bang' and contemporary ideas on the origin of matter, and of the Universe. He knew matter must come from somewhere and the theistic explanation was as valid as any other. As for the 'development hypothesis', this was alluding to thoughts on evolution that were an important conversation point in scientific circles in the mid-1850s, at the time when Henry was attending meetings of Learned Societies.

The case against the reality of the macro-chronology begins with the statement that: 'The course of nature is a circle', which Henry clarifies with several examples. The first is of a runner bean growing in his garden: the bean gives rise to cotyledons, a shoot, stem, [leaves], flower bud, flower, carpel, pod, and bean. His next example is that of a Lady Fern: spores produce a prothallus, sporal frond, tuft, caudex, fertile frond, sorus, theca and spores. From the Animal Kingdom comes the example of a Hawk moth: an egg gives rise to a larva, pupa and moth which then lays eggs. The examples continue with *Plumularia*, a marine hydrozoan or 'sea bristle' with polyps producing capsules from which planula larvae emerge, then a 'primal cell', axis, branch, and more polyps. Henry's final example is of a cow which produces an ovum, germinal vesicle (fertilised egg), embryonic vesicle, embryo, foetus, calf, heifer and cow. These are examples of the life cycles that are fundamental to Gosse's subsequent theory. The theory is best quoted in full, as it appears in *Omphalos*:

This, then, is the order of all organic nature. When once we are in any portion of the course, we find ourselves running in a circular groove, as endless as the course of a blind horse in a mill. It is evident that there is no one point in the history of any single creature, which is a legitimate beginning of existence. And this is not the law of some particular species, but of all: it pervades all classes of animals, all classes of plants, from the queenly palm down to the protococcus, from the monad up to man: the life of every organic being is whirling in a ceaseless circle, to which one knows not how to assign any commencement, – I will not say any certain or even probable, but any *possible*, commencement. The cow is as inevitable a sequence of the embryo, as the embryo is of the cow. Looking only at nature, or looking at it only with the lights of experience and reason, I see not how it is possible to avoid one of these two theories, the development of all organic existence out of gaseous elements, or the eternity of matter in its present forms … Creation, however, solves the dilemma. I have, in my postulates, begged the fact of creation, and I shall not, therefore attempt to prove it. Creation, the sovereign fiat of Almighty Power, gives us the commencing point, which we in vain seek in nature. But what is creation? It is the *sudden bursting into a circle*. Since there is no one stage in the course of existence, which more than any other affords a natural commencing point, whatever stage is selected by the arbitrary will of God, must be an un-natural, or rather a preter-natural, commencing point.

Henry continues by introducing his crux argument: all organisms which have had an actual existence are **diachronic** while those that appear to have existed previous 'to the violent act of creation' are **prochronic**. Organisms which are prochronic may be represented at any point in the circle of their life cycle and may show wear and tear, include gut contents, and have produced faeces and footprints. We infer that the events, both geological and biological, described in the evidence for the macro-chronology as occurring during agreed geological time scales, were really prochronic and were created at the same time as all the living, diachronic creatures and contemporary substrata.

As Henry has now untied the geological knot, the tone of the book changes and he wants to pass on his personal revelation. He does so with his characteristic enthusiasm and is almost euphoric. We commence an imaginary journey to examine Natural History immediately after the moment of the Creation, concentrating on the varied forms of plants and animals and describing their life cycles. The opening of this long section of 207 pages begins:

Since every organism, considering it, throughout its generations, as an unit, has been created, or made to commence existence, it is manifest that it was created or made to commence existence at some moment of time. I will ask some kind geological reader to imagine that moment, and to accompany me in an ideal tour of inspection among the creatures, taking up each for examination at the instant that it has been called into existence. Do not be alarmed! I am not about to assume that the moment in question was six thousand years ago, and no more; I will not rule the actual date at all; you, my geological friend, shall settle the chronology just as you please, or, if you like it better, we will leave the chronological date out of the inquiry, as an element not relevant to it. It may have been six hundred years ago, or six thousand, or sixty times six millions; let it for the present remain an indeterminate quantity. Only please to remember that the date *was* a reality, whether we can fix it or not; it *was* as precise as the moment in which I write this word.

The message is repeated for each organism seen in whatever life stage, and the enthusiasm is maintained for page after page. It now ceased to be a trial; rather it is a celebration of a case won, and Henry is just piling up all the examples that provide his concept of proof.

It does leave readers with questions. For example, the Laws section describes the life cycle of cows, yet Henry must have been aware that cows, while of one species, have been bred to produce many varieties. In addition, wild horses are discussed at the moment of their creation, but Henry must have been aware also of the varieties of horse, from miniatures to heavy horses, that have been bred from wild ancestors. The changes occurred by selective breeding of domestic stock by humans and, while it is possible technically for different varieties to interbreed, they are usually prevented from doing so. Some would not be able to because of differences in size and the same arguments could be made for breeds of dogs. This is not evidence of evolution by natural selection, of course, but Henry must have wondered what processes were involved in producing these varieties from wild type stock. Perhaps he thought that varieties were just a by-product of domestication?

Further questions arise when considering organisms with complex life cycles or in the strong association between individuals of different species. Tapeworms are examples of organisms that have complex life cycles involving primary and secondary hosts and, in *Omphalos*, Henry uses the tapeworm *Taenia* living in the gut of a panther as a case in point. He must have pondered how such a complex and essential association of life cycles between organisms came about, but there is little evidence of this thinking in *Omphalos*, dominated as it is by the theory of the prochronic. In his example, Henry writes that a segment of the tapeworm was excreted in the faeces of the panther and passed on to surrounding vegetation. Eggs from the segment were then eaten by a grazing antelope where metamorphosis resulted in eventual transport to the liver where a cyst (cysticercus) was formed. It was this cyst in the liver that was eaten by the panther and, after further metamorphosis, the adult tapeworm attached to the gut and began growing, then shedding mature segments to be excreted with the faeces:

Such is the "strange eventful history" of this repulsive creature; a history legitimately deducible, in all its stages, from its presently-existing condition. But it is a history altogether illusory. The *Taenia* never was a *Cysticercus*: the Panther is as yet guiltless of capricide: it is this moment called into being, and the Tapeworm begins existence within it.

To Henry, complex life cycles of this kind just came into existence through creation. They could not result from associations between organisms that then changed in subtle ways to produce a dependence of one on the other or, in the case of symbioses, mutual interdependence.

In the final section of his cross examination, Henry writes:

If it were legitimate to suppose that the first individual of the species Man was created in the condition answering to that of a new-born infant, there would still be the need of maternal milk for its sustenance, and maternal care for its protection, for a considerable period; while, if we carry on the suggested stage to the period when this provision is no longer indispensable, the development of hair, nails, bones, &c., will have proceeded through many stages. And, in either condition, the navel cord or its cicatrix remains, to testify to something anterior to both.

The comment on maternal care in this quote may have been a painful reminder to Henry of the death of Emily, but he took ordinarily a cold and objective approach to such things in his writings. The latter part of the quotation gives us the explanation for the title of the book. *Omphalos* is Ancient Greek for navel and alludes to the question, 'Did Adam have a navel if he had no mother?'

There are so many examples in the many pages of 'Parallels and Precedents', with organisms having both simple and complex life cycles. All of the organisms had been created a few minutes before the imaginary observer saw them and any features that were clearly of earlier forms were the result of a prochronic existence for that part of the life cycle. Everything depends on Henry's belief in his insight. At times, he seems over-enthusiastic, and Stephen Jay Gould in his essay *Adam's Navel* [3] describes the writing of this section of *Omphalos* as being in 'gloriously purple prose', and it seems very long, with an over-use of the word 'yonder'. There is no doubt that Henry, in his revelatory excitement wishes to hammer home the point, while seemingly oblivious of the extent of the reaction he was likely to provoke.

That said, there are signs that Henry was aware that there might be opposition to his theory of prochronic existence. In the conclusion to *Omphalos*, he defends himself against the view that the presence of fossils (of organisms that had no existence) indicates that The Creator was trying to deceive us:

It may be objected, that, to assume the world to have been created with fossil skeletons in its crust, – skeletons of animals that never really existed, – is to charge the Creator with forming objects whose sole purpose was to deceive us. The reply is obvious. Were the concentric timber-rings of a created tree formed merely to deceive? Were the growth lines of a created shell intended to deceive? Was the navel of the created Man intended to deceive him into the persuasion that he had a parent?

This defence is clearly weak, but Henry was right to suspect that this objection would be raised. If one believes that geological time is real, and that the Earth is more than 4 billion years old, and the oldest fossilised forms of life more than 3 billion years old, the idea of prochronic existence is absurd. Add to that the notion of evolutionary change and we can see how far Henry is removed from our contemporary view. But is he? There are still many who believe in the Biblical Creation and that days in Genesis mean real, 24-hour days, and that everything came into being a few thousand years ago. I don't know whether these believers have the insight that Henry used to overcome a conflict in his mind, resulting in the concept of prochronic existence. He knew that geological time was real, so had to invent this ingenious explanation to fit with Genesis. Biblical truth could not be questioned.

Henry also lets slip the following statement in his conclusion to *Omphalos*:

We have reason to believe that species die out, and are replaced by other species, like the individuals which belong to the species, and the organs which belong to the individual ... if we could take a sufficiently large view of the whole plan of nature, should we discern that the existence of species δ necessarily involved the pre-existence of species γ, and must inevitable be followed by species ε?

Some may feel that he is alluding to evolution here, but we know he was not. It is ironic that Darwin published his profound work *On the Origin of Species by Means of Natural Selection, or the Preservation of Favoured Races in the Struggle for Life* [4] just two years after the publication of *Omphalos*. How extraordinary it would have seemed to have the two books sitting side by side on a shelf of contemporary works by noted scientists and Fellows of the Royal Society.

Henry, recently bereaved after Emily's painful illness, with a young son, and an increasing reluctance for contact with colleagues in the Learned Societies, finished *Omphalos* with the following statements:

Here I close my labours. How far I have succeeded in accomplishing the task to which I bent myself, is not for me to judge. Others will determine that; and I am quite sure it will be determined fairly, on the whole. To prevent misapprehension, however, it may be as well to enunciate what the task was, which I prescribed, especially because other (collateral, hypothetical) points have been mooted in these pages All, then, that I consider myself responsible for is summed up in these sentences:-

I. The conclusions hitherto received have been but inferences deduced from certain premises: the witness who reveals the premises does *not* testify to the inferences.

II. The process of deducing the inferences has been liable to a vast incoming of error, arising from the operation of a *Law*, proved to exist, but hitherto unrecognised.

III. The amount of the error thus produced we have no means of knowing; much less of eliminating it.

IV. The whole of the facts deposed to by this witness are irrelevant to the question; and the witness is, therefore, out of court.

V. The field is left clear and undisputed for the one Witness on the opposite side, whose testimony is as follows:-

"IN SIX DAYS JEHOVAH MADE HEAVEN AND EARTH, THE SEA, AND ALL THAT IN THEM IS."

Reactions to Omphalos and Henry's need to incorporate his religious views into his writing

Henry expected a strong, positive response to *Omphalos*, such was his excitement at solving the conflict between geological time and the time given for The Creation in Genesis. He had organised a large initial printing of 4000 copies, but the book sold slowly and Freeman and Wertheimer in their bibliography of Gosse's work, conclude that many must have been pulped. They also suggest that, of all Henry's works published on a profit-sharing basis, this was the only one to show a loss. Edmund was of the opinion that, had Emily still been alive, she may have counselled against publication:

> He might probably have been content to leave others to fight out the question [of the Biblical account of Creation] on a philosophical basis, and might himself have quietly continued observing facts, and noting his observations with his early elegance and accuracy.

Given Henry's strong religious beliefs, which were certainly not to be compromised by any debate that conflicted with the Biblical account of Creation, I think it is unlikely that he could be stopped. It was his mission to write *Omphalos*.

Even in 1857, the idea of prochronic existence must have seemed very strange and one can only imagine the further jolt provided two years later by Darwin's *On the Origin of Species*. Darwin's ideas were much more exciting to emerging science, and to the wider intellectual community. An indication of the attitude towards Henry Gosse and *Omphalos* after the publication of Darwin's Origin in 1859 can be inferred from a comment given by David M. Knight in *Natural Science Books in English 1600-1900*:

While [Asa] Gray and [Alfred Russel] Wallace accepted Darwinism with qualification, Louis Agassiz, the Swiss-born geologist who added the ice ages to the geological calendar, remained like Owen an adamant opponent. In 1857 he began to publish his magnificently illustrated *Contributions to the Natural History of the United States*, where he was then living; and in 1859 the major part of the first volume was printed separately as an *Essay on Classification*. It represents the last appearance of the idealism of Cuvier's school; and is extraordinarily theological, rhetorical, and old-fashioned beside Darwin's work. Even odder is Philip [Henry] Gosse's *Omphalos* of 1857, urging that just as Adam would have been created with a navel, so the world was a recent creation filled with fossils of animals which had never lived. This Gosse was the father in Edmund Gosse's *Father and Son*, and a well-known naturalist. [5]

We get a flavour of the way the contemporary scientific establishment viewed Henry from the Obituary notice in the Proceedings of the Royal Society, an honour afforded to all deceased Fellows. [6]

The obituary for Darwin, who had died in 1882, covers the first twenty-five pages of the notices in volume 44. It is beautifully written by T. H. Huxley, who was in no doubt as to Darwin's significance. The obituary for Gosse was not only very much shorter but lacked flair and, predictably, did not mention *Omphalos*. After a brief description of Henry's early career in Canada, Alabama and Jamaica, the obituarist, Henry Bowman Brady, the expert on Foraminifera, notes that Henry collected marine plants and animals and, 'simultaneously perhaps with the late Mr. Warrington [sic.], devised the marine aquarium.' The obituary closes with an incorrect date for Henry's death and it is a sad effort although, in fairness, it does describe some of Henry's scientific works, while stressing his importance to the study of Natural History. A comparison of the length of the two pieces reflects the contemporary status of the two Fellows. It would become even more skewed as Darwin became a super-hero and

Gosse forgotten. How ironic that they should have shared the same volume of obituary notices.

Of recent commentators, Stephen Jay Gould is rather scathing in *Adam's Navel* and, like most scientists, he found Henry's ideas of prochronic existence nonsensical. Yet, Gould also recognised that Henry Gosse was 'a serious and fascinating man, not a hopeless crank or malcontent.' It is so much easier to dismiss a crank and it is good to see Henry accorded his true status by a fellow eminent communicator. Edmund describes *Omphalos* as being 'fatal' to Henry's scientific reputation, although several books of Natural History, and the distinguished *Actinologia Britannica* and *The Rotifera* (with Hudson), were published after *Omphalos*. Henry also published 51 scientific papers from 1857, ten appearing in 1858 alone. Whatever the reaction to *Omphalos*, all these papers further cemented his reputation as a careful observer of plants and animals.

If this was the attitude towards *Omphalos* amongst the secular and scientific community, what was the response of religious groups and individuals? It might have been expected that the book was better received in this quarter, but it was not. Edmund believes this disappointed Henry more than the response of the scientists. Then, as now, believers gave significance to The Great Flood of Noah's time as the major event which resulted in the sedimentation of minerals, and the mass death and fossilisation of plants and animals. There were Christians who did not share this view, but they were probably in a minority: Henry appears to have been one of these. His friend Charles Kingsley wrote to Henry on 4 May 1858, months after the publication of the book, that he was 'staggered and puzzled' by *Omphalos*. Like all serious readers of the work, he admired Henry's brave attempt at resolving the conflict between geological and Biblical time, but was perturbed by the idea that evidence of prochronic existence provided by fossils, and by Adam's navel, suggested that God is deceptive and could not therefore be a God of Truth. He clearly didn't back Henry's defence made in *Omphalos* against this accusation. Kingsley wrote: 'I cannot give up the painful and slow conclusion of five and twenty years' study of geology, and believe that God has written on the rocks one enormous and superfluous lie for all mankind.' He further suggests that Henry had given the Vestiges of Creation theory 'the best shove forward it has ever had.' This comment is a reference to *Vestiges of the Natural History of Creation* (published anonymously in 1844, but known to be the work of Robert Chambers), a book which supported the idea of extinctions and that the current structure of the Earth, both geological and biological, had developed from earlier forms, changing by means of natural numerical 'laws' defined by The Creator. In the anonymous author's words it was 'the first attempt to connect the natural sciences into a history of creation.' As with *Omphalos* thirteen years later, there was much opposition to *Vestiges of the Natural History of Creation* from both conservative scientists and clergymen but, unlike Henry's book, it was popular with the public and ran to many editions. It sold over 30,000 copies and its popularity at the time may have fuelled Henry's optimism for sales of *Omphalos* and encouraged him to place a large print order.

In his critique, Kingsley also focuses on the conclusion of *Omphalos* which could be taken as indicating that evolution was a likely explanation for the appearance of species. Kingsley urged Henry to address this in future editions and felt that he could be taken as supporting the transmutation of species theory of Lamarck. He wrote: 'I would not for a thousand pounds put your book into my children's hands.' That was the response of a close friend and, at the time, a fellow and absolute believer in Creation as described in Genesis. Opposition also came from one of the most loyal of Henry's family members. In *Glimpses of the Wonderful*,[7] Ann Thwaite mentions that even his devoted brother William, who had welcomed Henry to Newfoundland, changed his attitude to him in the light of all the poor reviews. Reactions to *Omphalos* from all sides are likely to have hurt Henry badly and the conflict between Creationists and the developing ideas in science were far from resolved, as he had intended them to be. Rather, the conflict was enhanced but, such was the nature of Henry's Christian beliefs, there could be no compromise. He was aware constantly that the End of the World was imminent, so his belief in a literal view of the Bible was paramount if he was to ascend to Heaven in rapture. Freeman and Wertheimer reprinted an advertisement for a sixteen page pamphlet written by Gosse in 1866, and entitled *Geology or God; Which? A supplement to 'Omphalos'*. No copies exist, but Freeman and Wertheimer suggested it was based on a letter written by Gosse to Kingsley in 1858 as a riposte to Kingsley's letter and comments.

An indication of the singular importance of Henry's religious beliefs and the feelings he must have had to the reception of *Omphalos* can be found by comparing the closing sections of two of his books: *A Naturalist's Sojourn in Jamaica* (1851, six years before *Omphalos*) and *A Year at the Shore* (1865, eight years after *Omphalos*). In *A Naturalist's Sojourn in Jamaica*, Henry, who has given his usual vivid descriptions of all that fascinates and absorbs him about Nature concludes with the following reflection:

Here I take a respectful leave of my readers and of tropical natural history together. If I have succeeded in imparting to the former a small portion of the delight, admiration, and enthusiasm, which invest in my own feelings the things I have essayed to present to them, I shall not have lost my labour. Eminently pleasing that labour has been: the compiling of these pages from my journals and papers, and from the correspondence of my beloved and honoured friend, has recalled in vivid power the lovely Eden-like scenes through which I wandered, and has made me live over again those months of unwearying delight that I spent in beauteous Jamaica. I can echo with fullest truth the experience of Bishop Heber: - "In every ride I have taken, and in every wilderness in which my tent has been pitched, I have found enough to keep my mind from sinking into the langour and the apathy which have been regarded as natural to a tropical climate." Nay, I may truly say, I found no *tendency* to apathy or ennui; every excursion presented something to admire; every day had its novelty; the morning was always pregnant with eager expectation; the evening invariably brought subjects of interest fresh and new; and the days were only too short for enjoyment. They were not days of stirring adventure, of dangerous conflicts with man or beast, of hair-breadth escapes in flood and field; their delights were calm and peaceful, I trust not unholy, nor unbecoming the character of a Christian, who has his heart in heaven, and who traces, even in earth's loveliest scenes, the mark of the Spoiler. The sentiments expressed on this subject by my friend and fellow-labourer [Hill, also a devout Christian] are those which I would ever associate with the study of science. "If the sight of nature," observes Mr. Hill, "were merely the looking at a painted pageantry, or at a spectacle filling the carnal mind with wonder and delight, the spirit would be overpowered and worked into weariness, but it is admiration at the wisdom, and reverence for the beneficence of Almighty power. He who 'dwelleth in the light which no man can approach unto; whom no man hath seen, nor can see,' is yet visible in his perfections through the works of his hand, and his designs are made manifest in the purpose of his creatures. Wherever our lot is cast, into whatever scenes our wayward impulses lead us, the mind-illumined eye gazes on divine things, and the spirit-stirred heart feels its pulses bounding with emotions from the touch of an ever-present Deity. The habit that sees in every object the wisdom and the goodness as well as the power of God, I may speak of, as Coleridge speaks of the poetical spirit, "It has been to me an exceeding great reward; it has soothed my afflictions; it has multiplied and refined my enjoyments; it has endeared my solitude; and it has given me the habit of wishing to discover the good and the beautiful in all that meets and surrounds me." ... GREAT ARE THY WORKS, JEHOVAH! INFINITE THY POWER! WHAT THOUGHT CAN MEASURE THEE, OR TONGUE RELATE THEE? ... FINIS.

Contrast that with the conclusion of Henry's *A Year at the Shore*:

I cannot conclude this volume without recording my solemn and deliberate protest against the infidelity with which, to a very painful extent, modern physical science is associated. I allude not only to the ground which the conclusions of modern geologists take, in opposition to the veracity of the "God which cannot lie," though the distinct statements which He has made to us concerning Creation are now, as if by common consent, put aside, with silent contempt, as effete fables, unworthy of a moment's thought, and this too before vast assemblages of persons, not one of whom lifts his voice for the truth of God. These assaults are at least open and unmasked. But there is in our scientific literature, and specially in that which takes a popular form, a tone equally dangerous and more insidious. It altogether ignores the awful truths of God's revelation, that all mankind are guilty and condemned and spiritually dead in Adam; that we are by nature children of wrath; that the whole world lieth in the wicked one; and that the wrath of God abideth on it: it ignores the glorious facts of atonement by the precious blood of Christ, and of acceptance in Him. It substitutes for these a mere sentimental admiration of nature, and teaches that the love of the beautiful makes man acceptable to God, and secures His favour. How often do we see quoted and be-praised, as if it were an indisputable axiom, the sentiment of a poet who ought to have known better,–

He prayeth best who loveth best
All things, both great and small;' –

a sentiment as silly as it is unscriptural; for what connexion can there be between the love of the inferior creatures, and the acceptableness of a sinner praying to the Holy God? It is the intervention of Christ Jesus, the anointed Priest, which alone gives prayer acceptance ... There is no sentimental or scientific road to heaven. There is absolutely nothing in the study of created things, however single, however intense, which will admit sinful man into the presence of God, or fit him to enjoy it. If there were, what need was there that the glorious Son, the everlasting Word, should be made flesh, and give His life a ransom for many? ... If I have come to God as a guilty sinner, and have found acceptance, and reconciliation, and sonship, in the blood of His only-begotten Son, then I may come down from that elevation, and study creation with advantage and profit; but to attempt to scale heaven with the ladder of natural history, is nothing else than Cain's religion; it is the presentation of the fruit of the earth, instead of the blood of the Lamb ... This will be, in all probability, the last occasion of my coming in literary guise before the public: how can I better take my leave than with the solemn testimony of the Spirit of God, which I affectionately commend to my readers, – ...THERE IS NO WAY INTO THE HOLIEST BUT BY THE BLOOD OF JESUS. FINIS.

The second of these extracts indicates to me a sense of hurt. Henry was becoming vengeful (on behalf of God), although it is likely that he would never have seen it that way.

Another example of the conflict between Henry's religious views and the world of science came in an exchange with the Council of the Linnean Society. Henry was interested in the developing career of Ray Lankester who, in turn, encouraged Henry, now in his early seventies, to write up his observations and drawings of the clasping organs of male Lepidoptera. Henry did not attend the meeting of the Royal Society in 1882 to give his paper, so an abstract was read by Huxley. However, the subject was not considered to be of wide interest, and subsequently was not published in the *Proceedings of the Royal Society*. Instead, it was submitted to the Linnean Society, with the Royal Society contributing £50 towards printing and engraving costs. As was usual in his publications, Henry included a paragraph of his religious thoughts and the Council of the Linnean Society felt that this was inappropriate. The Secretary asked Henry if he would remove the paragraph, as the Society could not include 'contentious matter on the subject of religion.' Of course, Henry refused, but Lankester intervened at this point and argued that Henry's paragraph would set a precedent whereby an atheist could then use the *Transactions* to support their religious interpretation (how typical of someone holding a Chair at UCL, known as 'The Godless University', to come up with such an argument). Henry could see the point that Lankester was making and acceded, reluctantly, to the request.

Henry's solely religious writing

Henry wrote many books and papers on religious topics, in addition to his publications in Natural History and Science. The evangelical tracts written by Emily and some co-written by Henry were collected as *Narrative Tracts* and published by Morgan and Chase in 1864. Among Henry's religious books are: *Monuments of Ancient Egypt, and their relation to the word of God* (1847); *Sacred streams: the ancient and modern history of the rivers of the Bible* (1850); *The history of the Jews, from the Christian era to the dawn of the Reformation* (1851) and A*ssyria; her manners and customs, arts and arms; restored from her monuments* (1852). All serve to link archaeological artefacts and Biblical history and their content and, may one say, evolution, are described by Freeman and Wertheimer. Fourteen years after this quartet, Henry published two short books: *The 6000 years of the world's history now closing: a table of scripture chronology, with notes* (1866) and *The Revelation: how is it to be interpreted?* (1866), both attuned to his apocalyptic view, shared by many other Christians at that time and, apparently, still today. His final large religious work was *The mysteries of God: a series of expositions of holy scripture* which appeared much later (1884). In addition to these works, a complete list of Henry's religious books should also include those on a wide range of biological subjects and on Natural History which were published by SPCK (The Society for Promoting Christian Knowledge). These were intended largely for a Christian audience or for a readership likely to be interested in a Christian perspective.

In addition to books, there were also many articles in religious journals. The year 1852 saw eight contributions to the *Weekly Visitor* on topics ranging from the Fall of Jericho, through Jesus at Jericho to the Serpent in the Wilderness. Thirty articles appeared in the *Christian Annotator* from 1854 to 1856 and these were on very short sections of Biblical text, often of just one verse. Henry spent hours poring over his Bible and this period was one where both he and Emily were seemingly at their most evangelical. There was a pause in the publication of articles during Emily's final illness and death, and also while *Omphalos* and the *Memorial* were being written. Henry then returned to writing religious articles in 1859 and 1860, with twelve in the *Bible Reader's Journal*. Perhaps in the light of the reception of *Omphalos* and his hardening view towards non-believers (and, by now, evolutionists), these included his thoughts on large-scale religious issues. These were: The present place of the believer beyond death and judgement; On sinning willfully; and replies to Remission of sins and Praying for the Holy Spirit. Two articles appeared in *Rainbow* in 1866 entitled On prophetic interpretation and Futurist principles examined. His final religious papers were Adam's federal headship (*Christian* 1883) and [The doctrine of] Limited election (*Christian* 1885).

If we add these religious publications to those on Natural History and on Science, we have confirmation of Henry as an industrious author and scholar, as well as a great field naturalist. His love of literature, especially poetry, also stimulated his romantic and artistic side and led to two books that show us all of Henry's interests combined: *The Romance of Natural History [First Series]* and *The Romance of Natural History [Second Series]*. Both were published by Nisbet & Co and written within four years of the publication of *Omphalos*. One would expect them to have been rather retaliatory and angry, in the manner of the conclusion of *A Year at the Shore* (1865) quoted earlier, but they were not.

The Romance of Natural History

Henry returned enthusiastically to Natural History when he settled in St Marychurch in September 1857, weeks before the publication of *Omphalos*. He was collecting from the shore and from other places, and making the observations which led to the publication of *Evenings at the Microscope* in 1859. *The Romance of Natural History [First Series]* is likely to have been published in the autumn of 1860 at the time he met Eliza, with *The Romance of Natural History [Second Series]* following in 1861, after their marriage. *The Second Series* is regarded generally to be inferior to the *First Series* and Henry's focus may have been distracted by his new-found happiness. Edmund commented in *The Naturalist of the Sea-Shore: The life of Philip Henry Gosse* that the *Second Series* 'suffers from the usual fate of continuation' and it was 'carried forth, rather too hastily, in consequence of the extraordinary popularity of the first'. It deserved to be extraordinarily popular as it shows Henry at his best, no doubt fuelled by the hurt and disappointment of the reactions to *Omphalos* and also by the recovery of his spirits, so evident after the move to Sandhurst. The scientific and religious debates of the day were put to one side as Henry returned to describing, in his engaging way, what he knew of many facets of the natural world.

The Preface to the *First Series* has a fascinating comment on Science and Natural History and the initial section is worth quoting:

There are more ways than one of studying natural history. There is Dr Dryasdust's way; which consists of mere accuracy of definition and differentiation; statistics as harsh and dry as the skins and bones in the museum where it is studied. There is the field-observer's way; the careful and conscientious accumulation and record of facts bearing on the life-history of the creatures; statistics as fresh and bright as the forest or meadow where they are gathered in the dewy morning. And there is the poet's way; who looks at nature through a glass peculiarly his own; the aesthetic aspect, which deals, not with statistics, but with the emotions of the human mind, – surprise, wonder, terror, revulsion, admiration, love, desire, and so forth, – which are made energetic by the contemplation of the creatures around him.

The first sentence mirrors Henry's comment in the Preface of *A Naturalist's Sojourn in Jamaica*, where he suggested that too much of the Biology of the time was based on preserved, rather than living plants and animals. We then have descriptions of Henry's love of observing organisms in their natural environment and the impact of his passion for Natural History on a more general aesthetic appreciation. Religious views are present, but the books are a celebration of an approach to Nature that, despite Henry's views, can stand on its own and provide satisfaction without the need for religious intrusion. They encourage the same sense of wonder in the natural world that I found supportive when experiencing tough times emotionally.

Henry writes that he always approached Natural History 'with a poet's heart' and this shows in the two volumes. While both contain some of Henry's best descriptive writing, the illustrations are mostly by Wolf, despite Henry's great skill as an illustrator. Freeman and Wertheimer identify the engravings resulting from Wolf's work in the *First Series* and the other two in this volume are from woodcuts by Henry. [8] One of the latter shows the unlikely 'Assault of a Cuttle' on a man standing near a rock pool, with a colleague running from the beach to his aid. It is a fine example of Victorian melodrama, and the notion must have appealed to Henry's mood of late 1860. I certainly find it great fun.

The wide-ranging, romantic approach is emphasised by the title of each chapter. In the *First Series*, one finds: 'Times and Seasons'; 'Harmonies'; 'Discrepancies'; 'Multum è Parvo'; 'The Vast'; 'The Minute'; 'The Memorable'; 'The Recluse'; 'The Wild'; 'The Terrible'; 'The Unknown', and 'The Great Unknown'. In

ASSAULT OF A CUTTLE.

X.

'Assault of a Cuttle', attributed to Gosse, *The Romance of Natural History [First Series]*,
P. H. Gosse, 1860.

the *Second Series*: 'The Extinct'; 'The Marvellous'; 'Mermaids';
'The Self-Immured'; 'Hybernation of Swallows'; 'The Crested
and Wattled Snake'; 'The Doubtful'; 'Fascination'; 'Serpent-
Charming'; 'Beauty', and 'Parasites.' Some of the chapter
headings are self-explanatory, others less so. The chapter 'Times
and Seasons', as would be expected, describes changes in
habitats through the year, and also the differences in the activity
of organisms in the night and during daylight. In contrast,
'Discrepancies' is used as a chapter heading 'for lack of a better',
and introduces us to extreme environments, like those of the
ocean deeps, snow and deserts. There are also seemingly fanciful
accounts of fishes living in boiling water and descriptions of the
blind fauna of caves. Henry writes that it has been suggested
that the latter have lost their eyes, having been descended from
sighted forms which earlier invaded the caves. He continues:

Mr Charles Darwin has lately alluded to these singular facts in confirmation of his theory of the origin of species by natural selection, or the preservation of favoured races in the struggle for life. He takes the view, that in the subterranean animals the organs of sight have become (more or less completely) absorbed, in successive generations, by disuse of the function.

True to his beliefs, Henry writes in a footnote to this section:

I am very far, indeed, from accepting Mr Darwin's theory to the extent to which he pushes it, completely trampling on Revelation as it does; but I think there is a *measure* of truth in it.

This is one step further towards thoughts on evolution than he took in *Omphalos* although, as was pointed out by Kingsley, there was that one paragraph which alluded to the idea, even though that was not Henry's intention. There are many references to Darwin in *The Romance of Natural History* and they are appreciative of his work, if not of his conclusions. While discussing the forests of Brazil, which he had not visited, Henry turns to the description provided by Darwin, acknowledging the impressions made of the forest on the latter's 'refined and poetic mind.' This shows further that Henry, whilst not accepting Darwin's views on evolution, applauded his sensitivity and ability as an observer of Natural History. He was characteristically generous to other Natural Historians.

Henry clearly enjoyed interpreting unusual phenomena, but was a stickler for accuracy in identification of animals and plants, just as in his biblical exegesis. Although he didn't have a lively imagination, the fanciful appealed to his poetic temperament and he was drawn to various fantastic stories. In *The Romance of Natural History [First Series]*, Henry stated:

The power of drawing correct inferences from what we see, and even of knowing *what we do really see*, and what we only *imagine* [Gosse's italics], is vastly augmented by the rigorous training of the faculties which long habits of observing certain classes of phenomena induce; and every man of science must have met with numberless cases in which statements egregiously false have been made to him in the most perfect good faith; his informant implicitly believing that he was simply telling what he had seen with his own eyes ... It is quite proper that, when evidence is presented of certain occurrences, the admission of which would overturn what we have come to consider as fixed laws, or against which there exists a high degree of antecedent improbability, – *that* evidence should be received with great suspicion. It should be carefully sifted; possible causes of error should be suggested; the powers of the observer to judge of the facts should be examined; the actual bounding line between sensuous perception and mental inference should be critically investigated; and confirmatory, yet independent, testimony should be sought. Yet, when we have done all this, we should ever remember that truth is stranger than fiction...

Another way in which the romance of natural history can be influenced by imagination comes with the anthropomorphic naming of objects. Henry gives an example of this when describing the giant redwoods of California, referred to as 'Mammoth Trees.' 'The Miner's Cabin' is a tree with a circumference of 80 feet and examples of other trees are 'The Three Graces', 'The Pioneer's Cabin', 'The Old Bachelor', 'The Father of the Forest' and 'The Mother of the Forest.' The Father has a circumference of 112 feet but has fallen, the trunk being at least 300 feet in length but broken, so the height in life must have been considerably more. Many of the trees are hollowed out or have 'cabins' burnt into them and the whole assemblage is thus an attraction, made more so by exhibitions of the bark of giant redwoods which were shown around the world as 'wonders.' Indeed, it was through exhibitions that Henry came to know of them. The anthropomorphic tree naming is furthered by Henry describing 'The Old Bachelor' as being 'a forlorn-looking individual'; 'The Hermit', 'rising solitary and alone', and 'The Old Maid', 'slightly bowing in her lonely grief.'

In *The Romance of Natural History [First Series]* is a section on 'Unearthliness' in which Henry writes:

The idea of *unearthliness* [Gosse's italics] is a great element in the Romance of Natural History. Our matter-of-fact age despises and scouts it as absurd, and those who are conscious of such impressions acknowledge that they are unreal, yet feel them none the less. The imaginative Greeks peopled every wild glen, every lonely shore, every obscure cavern, every solemn grove, with the spiritual, only rarely and fitfully visible or audible. So it has been with all peoples, especially in that semi-civilised stage which is so favourable to poetic developments; the elves and fays, the sprites and fairies, the Jack-o'-lanterns, the Will-o'-the-wisps, and Robin-goodfellows, and Banshees, – what are they all but the phenomena of nature, dimly discerned, and attributed by a poetic temperament to beings of unearthly races, but of earthly sympathies?

Here, Henry refers to the part played by brief sightings of natural events and organisms in the development of myths, a process that depends on imagination and elaboration. It is against this background that he discusses reports of creatures that may, or may not, be mythical, but his descriptions tend towards accepting their existence. It is all quite different to the meticulous observation, description and illustration for which Henry is famed.

In 'The Unknown', Henry describes, amongst other creatures, 'The Wild Man of America' and 'The Unicorn.' 'The Wild Man of America' is like a great ape, or human, and there have been sightings of such creatures in many parts of the world. Both native peoples and missionaries appeared to believe firmly in a wild man that was hairy, built huts and carried off women. Henry suggests that it was possible that there was some species of great ape that lived in South America, but he didn't extend this to belief in the attributes of hut building or abduction of women. As to the unicorn, Henry mentions that a South African zoologist, Dr Andrew Smith, both 'able and sober', collected information on a one-horned animal which could be placed zoologically somewhere between rhinoceroses and horses. There are numerous reports of such a creature from local villagers and, according to their descriptions the horn is flexible when the animal is at rest, becoming coiled when it is asleep. Then, when enraged, the horn becomes stiffened and is used in attack, doing damage to trees and to any humans that are encountered. Henry goes on to cite many other second-hand reports and also rock paintings that depicted not only antelopes of various kinds very accurately, but also unicorns. From the description of the nature of the horn, it is difficult not to conclude that it was not on the head of a mythical animal, but located elsewhere on its body. Perhaps near the rear legs, for example? Even if this explanation had occurred to Henry, it is very unlikely that it would have found its way into one of his books.

Sea Serpents

Sea serpents are given a chapter of their own, 'The Great Unknown', in *The Romance of Natural History [First Series]*. It follows a section on the 'Deep Sea' which concludes the previous chapter, 'The Unknown', as true a heading for the abyssal depths of the oceans today as it was then. However, a century and a half ago almost everything about the deep sea was unknown, although many eyes focused on the surface water of oceans from all the boats of different sizes involved in trade, fishing and the pursuit of power. Henry gives an amusing, but imagined, account of a mother talking with her seafaring son who had recounted seeing mountains of sugar, rivers of rum and flying fishes. She could accept the former two, but not flying fishes, as she knew they lived in the sea and not the air, so could not fly. In telling this story, Henry wanted to emphasise that many very unlikely biological phenomena exist. Of these, sea serpents seem especially interesting to him, even though all the sightings were made by others.

Henry sifts through the numerous descriptions of sea serpents and these are given below, in the order in which they appear in his narrative. He begins with those from Norway, where accounts included sightings by priests. It seems that sea serpents are deemed a feature of these northern latitudes, and the rich mythical culture of Scandinavia may flavour some of the descriptions. They 'stretched on the surface [of the sea] in receding coils or undulations, with the head, which resembles that of a horse, elevated some two feet out of the water.' Other observers described the head as being the 'size of a ten-gallon cask' and either pointed or rounded but there was general agreement that the serpent had 'large and glaring' eyes and a dark body. A flowing mane was only seen by some.

Next come reports from the north eastern coast of North America, where the serpents have a dark, mottled brown body with white under the head and neck, a reptilian head, and humps on the back, the whole animal being similar in size to a horse. Observers here also described the serpent's locomotion as being the result of vertical undulations of the body, a feature confirmed in a personal observation by a Colonel Perkins, who watched a serpent off Cape Ann in Massachusetts. His first sighting was some two miles offshore after which the animal swam near the harbour at Gloucester and he could see that its movement was not by the lateral undulations typical of a snake. The body of this serpent was chocolate brown in colour and it had a single horn on its head, and its sighting attracted a large crowd. Colonel Perkins went back to make more observations but there was no further appearance. He was able to speak to some residents of standing in the community and they reported the length of the serpent to be about a hundred feet and confirmed that it had a horn.

Henry then turns to the evidence of five British Army Officers who sailed from Halifax in what was to become Nova Scotia.

They intended to find good locations to fish for salmon and were on deck smoking cigars when they observed a large number of grampuses (Risso's dolphins or, perhaps, orcas) moving near them and, as military men on vacation, decided to fire at them with rifles. Their attention was then drawn to the explanation for the excitement in the grampuses; a large snake-like creature about eighty to one hundred feet in length with its head held clear of the water on a curved neck which had the thickness of a 'moderate-sized tree.' Like the other sightings, the body was dark brown in colour with streaks of white on the neck.

More evidence of the nature of sea serpents came from Captain M'Quhae of the frigate *HMS Daedalus*. A letter from M'Quhae was printed in *The Times* on 13 October 1848 in response to questions that had been raised by the Admiralty to a paragraph printed by the same newspaper on 9 October. This had recorded M'Quhae's sighting of a sea serpent on return from the East Indies; co-ordinates showing the location to be 500 km off the coast of what is now Namibia in south western Africa. As most serpents had so far been recorded from northern latitudes, this was thus a less usual Southern Hemisphere serpent. The letter is quoted in full by Henry and gives details of this animal. Its head ('without any doubt, that of a snake') was held at all times above the sea surface and its neck was about 15 inches in diameter, the whole serpent being at least sixty feet in length. It moved in a straight line but there was no obvious sign of how it moved, as it did not use undulations of the body. Consistent with other records, it was described as being dark brown in colour, with a yellowish white throat. There was no evidence of fins but it had a mane which resembled a mass of seaweed. M'Quhae provided a sketch of the serpent, later reproduced in the *Illustrated London News* on 28 October 1848. A separate description of the same animal was given in a diary kept by Lieutenant Drummond, the Officer of the Watch on *HMS Daedalus*. Unlike M'Quhae, Drummond described the animal as having a fin but their descriptions otherwise tally, both agreeing that it was dark brown and with lighter colouring on the throat or lower jaw. It reminded Drummond of a large snake or eel and the serpent was moving on a straight course, with the head kept horizontal to the sea surface, but dipping occasionally, and rapidly, into the water 'not apparently for purposes of respiration.' Drummond noted further that there was a sea running, so the squally conditions were stirring up the surface of the water.

Illustration of the Sea Serpent, *Illustrated London News*, 28 October 1848.

These colourful reports of sea serpents captured popular imagination and other observers began to describe their sightings as a result. Among these was Captain Beechey who stated that he had seen a large object in the South Atlantic and 'took it for the trunk of a large tree', but was not able to confirm this as it was lost from view before he could use binoculars. A further report was received from Mr Morries Stirling who was a director of a scientific society in Bergen; it was based on many sightings in Norwegian waters. Stirling ended his report to the Secretary of the Admiralty with a description of his own observations in smooth sea conditions when he was becalmed in a yacht. In distancing himself from the term sea serpent, Stirling describes a 'large fish or reptile of cylindrical form' about 30 feet in length and swimming using undulations.

Elaborating on M'Quhae's evidence of a lack of undulations and the carriage of the head and neck, 'F.G.S.', in a letter to *The Times* on 2 November 1848, suggested that the creature was a plesiosaur. He further suggested that the mane might resemble the neck coverings of some iguanas, thought to be related to the plesiosaurs. An opposing view was taken by Professor Richard Owen (later Sir Richard), the eminent palaeontologist and famous doubter of Darwin's theory of the origin of species by natural selection. He helped to found the Natural History Museum and had an incomparable knowledge of dinosaurs; indeed, he introduced the term. In Owen's opinion, M'Quhae's serpent was a seal. Owen opined that M'Quhae's drawing in the *Illustrated London News* showed the head was quite unlike that of a snake and the descriptions of the body surface suggest a covering of hair. Looking at all the evidence, and the location off south western Africa, Owen's opinion is that the sea serpent was an elephant seal, large individuals of which can grow over 20 feet in length, or it was perhaps another type of large seal. He further states that, should sea serpents be reptilian, it is odd that they are sighted only occasionally, despite being searched for, especially off the Norwegian coast.

M'Quhae replied to Owen refuting that the Serpent was a seal of any kind. He pointed out that its head was flattened, not vaulted and it really was about sixty feet in length as it swam near to the ship and was observed by many who were used to assessing the length of objects at sea. Further reports then came in to support M'Quhae's description, although one serpent was green with light spots rather than dark brown. This sighting was over 600 miles SE from the coast of South Africa, so a long way from shore. The serpent was described as being like an enormous snake with a crest like a saw. Other sightings were recorded from a similar location to that of M'Quhae's serpent and one of these came from Mr Merriman, the Master of the British ship *Brazilian* which was becalmed on a voyage out from the Cape of Good Hope. Having sighted a serpent, Merriman ordered the launch of a boat and, with three others, set off intending to harpoon it. On getting close, however, they found that this supposed serpent was a mass of floating seaweed with a huge holdfast that gave the impression of a crest. A further sighting of seaweed was made by Captain Fred Smith of the *Pekin* who made observations of the 'serpent' using a telescope, seeing its huge size, with the head and neck covered with a shaggy mane. A boat was launched and 'at length' they came close to the head. 'They seemed to hesitate, and then busy themselves with the line, the monster all the time ducking its head, and shewing its great length.' They came back to the *Pekin* and hoisted the monster aboard to find, like Merriman, that they had captured a mass of seaweed with the holdfast(s) giving the appearance of a head, and sea swells conveying a sense of movement to the mass. Without having dragged the seaweed on board for close examination, it is likely that Captain Smith would have stated it to be a serpent. Gosse concludes the evidence by returning to the account by an[other?] officer on *HMS Daedalus*, who re-affirmed that he had seen the head with many features, including eyes, nostrils, and mouth, and that the serpent was propelled by fins rather than undulations.

Being a Victorian Englishman, Henry confines his comments to the evidence provided by '*English* witnesses of known character and position, most of them being officers under the crown.' He begins with a summary of the characteristics of a sea serpent, based on observations:
1. It has the general form of a serpent
2. It has a great length, suggested to be more than sixty feet

3. The head resembles that of a reptile
4. The neck is up to sixteen inches in diameter
5. Although there is a considerable discrepancy in descriptions, it has a crest and / or mane
6. The Serpent is either dark brown, or green, in colour, but has light patches on the neck and head, or is streaked and spotted with white
7. It swims submerged with the neck and head protruding above the surface
8. The Serpent moves rapidly on a straight course
9. It is air-breathing and 'spouts in the manner of a whale'

Having earlier presented the observations and views of others on the explanation for sea serpents, Henry then uses the characteristics listed above in giving us his view. He goes through the possibilities, taking into account the views of Owen and others, and dismisses them in turn. He sides with those who suggest that sea serpents are reptiles and, probably, enaliosaurs (an extinct group of marine reptiles that includes the plesiosaurs). Henry argues his case using his knowledge of fossils and makes this interesting statement:

It must not be forgotten, as Mr Darwin has ably insisted, that the specimens we possess of fossil organisms are very far indeed from being a compete series. They are rather fragments accidentally preserved, by favouring circumstances, in an almost total wreck. The *Enaliosauria*, particularly abundant in the secondary epoch, may have become sufficiently scarce in the tertiary to have no representative in these preserved fragmentary collections, and yet not have been absolutely extinct.

Henry's whole account is rational and based on his knowledge of Palaeontology (a knowledge so evident in the first part of *Omphalos*), of Biology and of illustration. The conclusion that sea serpents are giant reptiles is reached by deduction from circumstantial evidence. From today's perspective it seems highly probable that Henry's conclusion was incorrect, but we do not know. Perhaps the most telling point about his discussion is a footnote to the quote about the fossil record given above. Henry wrote: 'I reason as a geologist, on geological premises, – reserving my own convictions on the subject of *prochronism*, which would not affect this argument.'

Accordingly, *The Romance of Natural History [First Series]* ends with a return from speculation on sea serpents to prochronism, the latter being very real to Henry. We get more on similar themes of the unlikely in the *Second Series* and it is difficult sometimes, but only sometimes, to believe the author possessed rigid beliefs in Biblical Creation.

Extinction, animals that fall from the sky, and mermaids

Henry alludes to extinctions in his discussion of sea serpents, and returns to the topic in the first chapter of *The Romance of Natural History [Second Series]*. Among the subjects that follow, and in which the poetic side of Natural History is evident, are the phenomenon of organisms falling in rain, in a chapter entitled 'The Marvellous', and mermaids, given a chapter of their own.

In the *First Series*, Henry makes reference to his prochronic theory when discussing the extinction of reptiles, and the first chapter in the *Second Series* sees him back to religious fervour, at least in the first few pages. The tone here is similar to that of his self-defence in *Omphalos*. After describing animals that have become extinct, like giant land tortoises, mammoths, and the moa, Henry goes on to consider the biology of extinction and the role played by contact with humans. Once one passes over the opening section, the chapter shows Henry is not only well-informed and well read in Biology, but also a clear thinker, if constrained by his own religious dogma. Henry was clearly influenced by contemporary thought about evolution and this must have been difficult for him. He puzzles as to why species become extinct; something which he finds 'possesses a very peculiar interest.' This statement follows an acceptance that new species may appear, but not through the process of evolution of one type into another. Rather, Henry has the concept of creation being continuous, after the tumultuous initial Creation of prochronic and diachronic life. It seems quite a step for him to make:

... Probability would suggest that new forms are continually created to supply the lack of deceased ones; and it may be that some, at least, of the creatures ever and anon described as new to science, especially in old and well-searched regions, may be newly called into being, as well as newly discovered. It may be so, I say; I have no evidence that it is so, except the probability of analogy; we know that the rate of mortality among individuals of a species, speaking generally, is equalled by the rate of birth, and we may suppose this balance of life to be paralleled when the unit is a species, and not an individual. If the Word of God contained anything either in statement or principle contrary to such a supposition, I would not entertain it for a moment, but I do not know that it does. I do not know that it is anywhere implied that God created no more after the six days' work was done. His Sabbath-rest having been broken by the incoming of sin, we know from John v. 17, that He continued to work without interruption; and we may fairly conclude that progressive creation was included as a part of that unceasing work.

It might be suggested that this is a convenient explanation in the light of an overwhelming body of opinion on the likelihood of evolution being the only logical explanation for new species. In opting for spontaneous generation of new forms, Henry was anchored in earlier views in Biology, but it was the only explanation that did not threaten his religious views. After *Omphalos*, it seems to be a compromise.

In the second chapter of *The Romance of Natural History [Second Series]* we read of some strange, even weird, natural events. These, of course, give rise to myths and that is a natural human reaction when rational explanation is difficult: sometimes, the rational also seems unbelievable. Henry begins with reports of red spots left by butterflies and his own observations of aggregations of red worms at the bottom of a pond in Devonshire. Both may look like drops of blood and could easily enter popular mythology as such, but clearly they are not. Red spots are also produced by the excreta of some birds, and Henry describes reports of red faeces produced by fish-eating Little Auks. A more general phenomenon of reddening is from the growth of red bacteria or algae in the waters of lakes and ponds, which convey an impression of blood gathering at, or near, the surface. It has been suggested that these organisms may explain one of the Ten Plagues of Egypt, where rivers were turned to blood, and the defensive Henry is quick to point out that, should this be the explanation, its rapid occurrence would require Divine power.

Another peculiar phenomenon is that of organisms falling in rain, and Henry gives the examples of fishes and amphibians. He does not provide explanations, nor does he mention an earlier description of frog eggs falling from the sky given by Moreau de St. Méry and which he quotes in *A Naturalist's Sojourn in Jamaica*. There are many documented cases of fishes and amphibians appearing in this way, as they are swept up by strong winds, or water spouts, and deposited elsewhere once the winds abate. Their fall is part of a natural, but strange, cycle of events. Henry then moves on to consider what happens to aquatic animals when their habitats dry, providing descriptions of the extraordinary lungfish which breathe air while buried in a cocoon at the bottom of dried water bodies, and he discusses the remarkable powers of some fish to cross land and even climb trees. These are marvellous adaptations, but it is in the next chapter, on Mermaids, that we return to his attempt to give rational explanations of the unbelievable.

Henry begins with reports of mermen from ancient times (over two thousand years ago), with Belosus describing a merman with its upper half human and its lower half fish, but also with feet that appeared to be attached to the tail. He points out that mythical creatures of this description occur in several cultures, including those of Scandinavia. Just as with sea serpents, Henry wonders whether the descriptions were of real aquatic organisms. As there was such a popular interest and long-held belief in mermen and mermaids, they became a feature of travelling shows and Henry recounts an experience of his own:

> In my boyhood I well recollect being highly excited by the arrival in our town, at fair-time, of a 'show', which professed to exhibit a mermaid, whose portrait, on canvas hung outside, was radiant in feminine loveliness and piscine scaliness. I fondly expected to see the very counterpart within, how disposed I did not venture to imagine, but alive and fascinating, of course. Had I not seen her picture? I joyfully paid my coppers, but oh! woful [*sic.*] disappointment! I dimly saw, within a dusty glass case, in a dark corner, a shrivelled and blackened little thing which might have been moulded in mud for aught I could see, but which was labelled, "MERMAID!" So great was my disgust, so bitter my feelings of shame and anger at having been so grossly taken in, that I did not care to observe what might have been noteworthy in it. I read afterwards that it was a very ingenious cheat; the trunk and head of a monkey had been grafted on to the body and tail of a large salmon-like fish, and the junction had been so cleverly effected, that only a very close examination detected the artifice ... the mermaids exhibited in Europe and America, to the great profit of the enterprising showmen, have all been of Japanese manufacture.

Hence, sightings of mermaids and mermen had these pre-conceived images superimposed upon them. If earlier observations of Sea Serpents were subject to interpretation by comparison with the familiar, so were mermaids, only the image was of the impossible. The question then arises of whether the myth extended from the observation of some unknown creature, quite unlike anything else in the Animal Kingdom.

Henry continues his narrative with a description of the popular source of the mermaid legend, that of dugongs and manatees. Both show strong maternal behaviour and suckle their calves while holding them with one flipper and, while diving, show the transverse tail fluke that has the same orientation as the tail of mermaids. Several other sightings were probably of seals, despite mermaid-like qualities which some observers swore to be accurate. There was one record to which Henry gives special focus: an account from observers known to Dr Robert Hamilton, the author of *History of the Whales and Seals*, and who Hamilton felt were reliable witnesses. They reported that a fishing boat off Yell in the Shetland Islands landed a mermaid which had become caught in its nets. It was about three feet long, had protuberant mammary glands, the face and neck of a monkey, arms folded across the chest with no webbing between the fingers, and the lower part of the body was that of a fish, perhaps like a dogfish. The skin was smooth and grey and there were spines on the head and neck which could be raised like a crest. Henry offers no explanation as to the identity of this creature and concludes by stating:

> On a review of the whole evidence, I do not judge that this single story is a sufficient foundation for believing in the existence of mermaids; but, taken into combination with other statements, it induces a strong suspicion that the northern seas may hold forms of life as yet uncatalogued by science.

There are further, perhaps lesser, chapters in *The Romance of Natural History [Second Series]*, but this account shows that Henry is not easily moved by mythology and conjecture when considering the identity of organisms. Unlike some, he is not afraid of discussing such creatures, and of strange natural phenomena, among the wonderful in Natural History and I share this inclination.

We have a picture of Henry Gosse as a man of many parts: deeply religious; delighted by the World and yet disenchanted by it; a caring father; a victim of his own shyness, and much else besides. Like many of us, he was thus a complicated man, but the most popular image of Henry is provided by Edmund in his second biography and autobiography *Father and Son*. [9]

1 Gosse, P. H., *A Memorial of the Last Days on Earth of Emily Gosse*, (James Nisbet and Co.), London, 1857.

2 Gosse, P. H., *Omphalos: an attempt to untie the geological knot*, (John Van Voorst), London, 1857.

3 Gould, S. J., *Adam's Navel and other essays*, (Penguin), London, 1995.

4 Darwin, C, *On the Origin of Species by Means of Natural Selection, or the Preservation of Favoured Races in the Struggle for Life*, (John Murray), 1859.

5 Knight, D. M., (1989) *Natural Science Books in English 1600-1900*, (Portman), London, 1989.

6 *Proceedings of the Royal Society, Vol 44, pp. xxvii - xxviii, 1888.*

7 Thwaite, A, *Glimpses of the Wonderful: The Life of Philip Henry Gosse*, (Faber and Faber), London, 2002.

8 Attribution of the illustrations by Wolf in *The Romance of Natural History [First Series]* is given by Freeman, R. B., and Wertheimer, D, *Philip Henry Gosse: A Bibliography*, (Dawson Publishing), Folkestone, 1980.

9 Gosse, E, *Father and Son. A Study of Two Temperaments*, (William Heinemann), London, 1907. Reprinted, (Penguin), London, 1986.

Henry and Edmund

Father and Son

No compromise, it is seen, was offered; no proposal of a truce would have been acceptable. It was a case of "Everything or Nothing"; and thus desperately challenged, the young man's conscience threw off once for all the yoke of his "dedication", and, as respectfully as he could, without parade or remonstrance, he took a human being's privilege to fashion his inner life for himself.

From *Father and Son*, by Edmund Gosse

*F*ather and Son, published seventeen years after Edmund Gosse's first biography of his father, is different from *The Naturalist of the Sea-Shore; The Life of Philip Henry Gosse*, as it describes Henry and family life, from Edmund's perspective.

The sometimes negative view of Henry presented may have fitted with the attitudes of Edmund's circle at the time, or it may reflect a sense of being hard done by. At this point, it is worth quoting Ann Thwaite in *Glimpses of the Wonderful*:

I wrote my biography of Edmund Gosse, realizing how little I could rely on what he wrote himself, however much I admired the way he said it ... [Henry] could be pious and earnest on occasion, but he was also enthusiastic, excited and endlessly curious. [1]

We need to remember this when reading *Father and Son*, for Edmund looks back at his upbringing from the viewpoint of a well-connected 57-year-old. Inevitably, there is an overlap of material between the two biographies and that is repeated to some degree here, but we need to know more about Edmund's thoughts, even though the record may not be entirely reliable. It is from the two biographies that we know most about Henry as a father and as a strongly-principled individual and, of course, we also know about Henry from his own books and letters, and those of others close to him. *Father and Son* was first published anonymously, going quickly through four further editions within the first year. Only after its success did Edmund admit to being the author and it became his most famous work.

Peter Abbs, the poet and student of the 'Self', provides valuable background information in his Introduction to the 1986 Penguin Twentieth-Century Classics edition of *Father and Son*. [2] He stresses that the book was well received by critics, especially in America, and pillars of the British literary establishment praised it. Abbs describes Edmund as finding in literature 'a refuge from the chilling demands of his puritanical background', emphasising the impression of Henry that sections of *Father and Son* created. Edmund's views are crystallised in a letter which he wrote to Robert Ross a great patron of the literary arts and close friend of Oscar Wilde, and which is included in Abbs' Introduction:

> I detest nothing so much as the *cliché* in mankind. And more and more personal liberty becomes a passion, almost a fanaticism with me. Less and less can I endure the idea of punishing a man – who is not cruel – because he is unlike other men. Probably if the hideous new religion of Science does not smother all liberty, we are in the darkness before the dawn of a humane and intelligent recognition of the right to differences.

This right to differences in all matters shapes Edmund's whole approach to his relationship with Henry as described in *Father and Son*. The account is claimed to be 'scrupulously true' and the only untrue aspects are the names of the main characters, as these have been changed. Edmund explains that this was to avoid offence, but that seems a little odd, especially as he preferred anonymity at the time of publication. Why was Edmund worried about causing offence? The Preface finishes with a statement that the book contains both comedy and tragedy and that ' ... those who are affected by the pathos of it will not need to have it explained to them that the comedy was superficial and the tragedy essential.'

Edmund begins by stressing that he and Henry never lost their respect for one another yet 'one [Henry] was born to fly backward, the other [Edmund] could not help being carried forward.' This, of course referred to the personalities and ambitions of father and son, but Edmund also alludes to their status:

My parents were poor gentlefolks; not young; solitary, sensitive and although they did not know it, proud. They both belonged to what is called the Middle Class, and there was this further resemblance between them that they each descended from families which had been more well-to-do in the eighteenth century, and had gradually sunken in fortune.

This is a further reflection of the position adopted by Edmund in this memoir; one almost of condescension. This extends to his description of Henry and Emily's religious beliefs and their moves from organised religious groupings into those of 'extreme Calvinists like themselves'. A further comment was that neither his father nor mother was interested in poetry after the age of Byron, and in the case of romantic fiction since the Waverley novels. All their leisure time was spent studying The Bible. This distance, coupled with Edmund's obvious feeling of not being wanted (' ... the advent of a child was not welcomed, but was borne with resignation'), leaves us in no doubt about Edmund's position when writing *Father and Son*. He wants to show how important he has become and to demean his father in the process. This view is reinforced by Edmund's description of his difficult birth, with all attention having been focussed on Emily after the delivery, while he was left, being revived by an 'old woman who happened to be there.' It is painful to read such an introduction, having come to know Henry through his writings and the descriptions in the earlier biography. There was a gulf between the two men and Edmund, from his vaunted position as a successful member of the Establishment, is determined to communicate this to the reader. That, and the oppression provided by his strict religious upbringing. He was to be kept 'unspotted by the world.'

Edmund appreciated the attentions of his mother but she, too, was so powerfully religious as to appear stifling to him on occasions. Her personal diary, from which Edmund quotes, has a note expressing her feeling that: 'We have given him to the Lord.' He spent much time with her while Henry was busy writing, drawing, collecting and working at the microscope, not caring about the 'praise of the learned world.' This was the daily routine of early family life in London, while on Sundays there were the meetings of the Brethren. Although both parents were totally subservient to the Will of God, Edmund felt that Emily was the stronger of the two strong characters and he confirms that she had a powerful influence on many of Henry's important decisions; for example, her death removed a brake on Henry's impulse to publish *Omphalos*. An isolated only child, Edmund showed no real wish to have playmates and all his social contacts were with adults.

Although she had been employed as a governess, Emily did not enjoy teaching and Henry taught Edmund 'cheerfully, by fits and starts.' He acknowledges both Henry's skill as a teacher and his ability to devise various schemes to aid learning, which were, in part, gained from his time as an innovative schoolmaster in Hackney. Nevertheless, attempts to make Edmund learn passages of scripture and other religious writings met with a block and this resistance both displeased and confused Henry. As an enthusiastic reader, Edmund, in turn, was perplexed by Emily's refusal to allow any works of fiction into the house, even those on religious topics. There were no bedtime readings for Edmund and no chance to read further when growing up. His reading he described as such:

... a queer variety of natural history, some of it quite indigestible by my undeveloped mind; many books of travels, mainly of scientific character, among them voyages of discovery in the South Seas, by which my brain was dimly filled with splendour; some geography and astronomy, both of them sincerely enjoyed; much theology, which I desired to appreciate but could never get my teeth into (if I may venture to say so), and over which my eye and tongue learned to slip without penetrating, so that I would read, and read aloud, and with great propriety of emphasis, page after page without having formed an expression ... Later on, a publication called *The Penny Cyclopaedia* became my daily, and for a long time almost my sole study...

Edmund was thus an avid and curious fact collector, just like his father. What is it which draws some of us to encyclopaedias and the wealth of information that they contain, and why is fact collection so absorbing? I suppose that it is no different to train spotting in some ways, yet using facts to marshal information into arguments seems worthwhile, whereas underlining numbers in a book does not. Edmund had another outlet for his curiosity to add to his study of *The Penny Cyclopaedia*. At the outbreak of the Crimean War, the Gosses took a daily newspaper for the first time and this widened Edmund's perspective, as he and Henry enjoyed discussions on some of the places mentioned, looking at maps to locate them.

After collecting visits to Devon and Dorset, the family returned to Islington and Henry was now being paid for his writing, so life was a little more comfortable. Henry was deferred to by

Emily and, of course, by Edmund. For Emily this was a matter of course; for Edmund a result of his position, which, typically in a growing child, he challenged when he realised that Henry was not omniscient: 'My father, as a deity, as a natural force of immense prestige, fell in my eyes to a human level. In future, his statements about things in general need not be accepted implicitly.' This observation is not, of course, unique to Edmund and is something we all discover about our parents as we grow up. Nevertheless, the discovery that he knew things, which his father did not, gave Edmund confidence in his own way of thinking. He began to develop fantasies based on his imaginary power to make animals come to life from pictures; to be able to sing very loudly while in the chapel; to be able to count numbers to find some secret. All common kinds of childish fantasy but, as Edmund did not have contact with other children, these thoughts must have had a special meaning for him. Of course, neither Henry nor Emily knew what was going on in Edmund's mind, but they were aware of physical evidence of turmoil, as he claims to have started self-harming by cutting as a test of his 'practical magic.' Such behaviour makes me wonder whether this was all part of the 'dual individuality' which he felt at the time, something that came to the fore after an hysterical outburst when Edmund would bash his head on a table while his other aloof persona watched? Even an amateur psychologist can see the conflict already welling up in Edmund and his testimony is very candid, given Edmund's position in society in 1907. Although psychoanalysis was being developed in the early twentieth century, there was not much social tolerance of mental health problems.

One night in bed, after saying his prayers with Emily, Edmund heard rustling sounds. To stop the noise he prayed 'very fervently to God to save me from my enemies' but, when this failed, he resorted to shouting. His parents rushed to comfort him and it was discovered that the rustling noise came from framed texts that were displaced in the draught created by the bedroom door being left ajar. A common enough event and all children are assured when there is a clear and rational explanation for such noises, even though they, like the rest of us, are somehow programmed to use their powers of imagination.

It was at this juncture in his young life that Edmund, in his childish way, was starting to pose questions about his parent's strict religiosity:

I had need of a large painted humming-top which I had seen in a shop-window in the Caledonian Road. Accordingly, I introduced a supplication for this object into my evening prayer, carefully adding the words: "If it is Thy will." This, I recollect, placed my Mother in a dilemma, and she consulted my Father. Taken, I suppose, at a disadvantage, my father told me I must not pray for "things like that." To which I answered by another query, "Why?" And I added that he said that we ought to pray for things we needed, and that I needed the humming-top a great deal more than I did the conversion of the heathen or the restitution of Jerusalem to the Jews, two objects of my nightly supplication which left me very cold ... I have reason to believe, looking back upon this scene, conducted by candle-light in the front parlour, that my Mother was much baffled by the logic of my argument. She had gone so far as to say publicly that no "things or circumstances are too insignificant to bring before the God of the whole earth." I persisted that this covered the case of the humming-top, which was extremely significant to me. I noticed that she held aloof from the discussion, which was carried on with some show of annoyance by my Father. He had never gone quite so far as she did in regard to this question of praying for material things. I am not sure that she was convinced that I ought to have been checked; but he could not help seeing that it reduced their favourite theory to an absurdity for a small child to exercise the privilege. He ceased to argue, and told me peremptorily that it was not right for me to pray for things like humming-tops and that I must do it no more.

It is another example of profound religious belief as a prison. A child's simple longing for a special toy, and the badgering of parents to ensure its purchase, becomes a serious issue, rather than one which can be readily de-fused. It all seems very sad and I am most grateful that my own religious upbringing never came remotely near such repression in the name of God. It was not just the brusque rejection of his son's wishes either. At about the time of his sixth birthday, Edmund disobeyed a particular request from Henry and this resulted in a caning. Looking back, Edmund concedes that this episode was driven by Henry's unpleasant religious belief that children should be beaten if they do wrong, and it was not the result of personal malice. Nonetheless, the effect was to make the son hate the father, understandably, for a short time, but this feeling passed, and warmth and harmony returned.

Like most children, Edmund was ready to tease as a way of expressing his independence. In one session of personal prayers, he pretended to worship a chair instead of using his normal form of address to the Almighty, addressing it as 'O Chair' every time 'O God' was normally required. Although Henry was likely to have been confused and angry at his son's behaviour, this test also left Edmund quaking with fear of God's retribution, but nothing came from on high and, deep down, he did not expect anything to happen. He concluded that God did not care about idolatry and this, of course, conflicted with Henry's views and lessened Edmund's respect for his father's beliefs even further. This imposition of religious dogma colours everything that follows in *Father and Son*. Henry's version of Christianity not only supported corporal punishment (a not unusual means of bringing children into line in the nineteenth century, as well as in the present) but also the bullying demand for acquiescence to a parent's interpretation of religious truth. It was indoctrination, but well meant.

Whatever the constraints, close family life was about to change forever. Edmund claims to have overheard his mother tell his father about the diagnosis of her breast cancer and he witnessed them embracing and then praying together. From this time, he relates that Emily continued her evangelical work, handing out tracts to people that she encountered, despite what he claims to be her natural timidity. This outgoing side of her nature was maintained during the visit to Tenby, and Emily clearly found it much easier to be open than did Henry, shown by her love of social contact when younger. Emily's illness and its treatment were not the only challenges facing the Gosse family at this time as there was also financial hardship. Emily's small inheritance had been invested in an unsuccessful Cornish mine so they were now dependent on the irregular income from Henry's books and lecturing. If these final, dreadful times for the Gosse family were not enough, further demands were brought upon Emily by her brothers' misfortunes. Her work as a governess, work which she did not like, had helped to pay for the brothers to complete courses at Cambridge. Now, both had fled to Paris to avoid their creditors, just when Henry was also in financial straits, and their plight did not receive much sympathy.

On return from Tenby, Edmund was living with his now very sick mother in lodgings near her doctor in Pimlico, as trips to consultations from the family home, where Henry continued to live and work, became exhausting. Edmund was thus a solo witness to Emily's pain and anguish and he was also her only support most of the time, taking pleasure in being able to arrange her pillows to make her slightly more comfortable. She had her faith to sustain her, of course, and her belief in the literal truth of The Bible, with everything taken on factual grounds without any caution in the interpretation of what was written. Emily's condition worsened, and mother and son returned to Islington, a marked change for Edmund as he was no longer the sole support for long periods and he did not have his mother's exclusive attention. He wrote tenderly of one of their last times together:

When the very end approached, and her mind was growing clouded, she gathered her strength together to say to my Father, "I shall walk with Him in white. Won't you take our lamb and walk with me?" Confused with sorrow and alarm, my Father failed to understand her meaning. She became agitated and she repeated two or three times: "Take our lamb, and walk with me!" Then my Father comprehended, and pressed me forward; her hand fell softly upon mine and she seemed content. Thus was my dedication, that had begun in my cradle, sealed with the most solemn, the most poignant and irresistible insistence, at the death-bed of the holiest and purest of women. But what a weight, intolerable as the burden of Atlas, to lay on the shoulders of a little fragile child!

This passage gives us a powerful insight into Edmund's love for his mother and her love for him; we also have another demonstration of the extraordinary power that religion held in that household. Although *Father and Son* was written many years later, it is clear that Edmund felt crushed by both this power and by Emily's death. The times spent with Emily in Pimlico were a trial in witnessing her deteriorating condition and physical pain, but there was compensation in their closeness. He didn't record whether he felt resentment at Henry's absence for much of the time, but surely there were times when he did. Henry had to earn money however, and needed to progress with his work, for even with his faith, twenty-four hours a day contact would have been almost unbearable and Edmund was at least able to sleep through the night.

Whilst I can relate to Edmund in losing a loving mother, his experience was very different to mine, as my mother died after a long spell in hospital, so I felt rather detached. There was no death-bed scene for me, although it was not pleasant to see Mum suffering in the last few visits I made to the hospital. Thus far, I therefore warm to both Henry and to Edmund but, as would be expected of such contrasting characters only to aspects of each.

After Emily's death, a distraught Henry had to earn money from a lecture tour of northern and central England, something that his fame as a Natural History writer, and as the inventor of the aquarium, had made possible. It must have been difficult for him, and no less so when Edmund could not be brought along. Fortunately, one of Henry's cousins had contacted him after Emily died and offered to look after Edmund with her own, large family in Clifton, Bristol whenever Henry was away. Although 'God-fearing', the family was not as strictly religious as Edmund's own and he was in the company of younger people for the first time, even though the children were rather older than him. Although he could remember little of the detail of his time in Clifton, Edmund recollects that it was more relaxed than his home surroundings, and the activity and general noisiness were just what he needed after the very tough time in London. It must have registered that there were different ways of living a Christian way of life and this must have encouraged him.

On moving back to Islington, Edmund found that time moved slowly and he most enjoyed watching the comings and goings along the street. Inside the house he continued to read avidly in *The Penny Cyclopaedia*, accumulating miscellaneous snippets of information on many topics. This no doubt served also as a diversion from the time spent with his father who, whilst still believing that the family would be reunited in Heaven, was grieving for Emily and only too aware of the situation that he found himself in as the father of a young son. The summer of 1857 was the time when Edmund felt that he and his father were closest, sharing their melancholy and ' ... we seldom spoke of what lay so warm and fragrant between us, the flower-like thought of our Departed.'

Unlike the jolly, distracting company of the Clifton cousins, which had helped Edmund to regain his spirits, life for father and son in Islington was shared between misery and study of the Bible. While not too mindful of its contents, Edmund became impressed with the language of the Epistle to the Hebrews, and he later wrote that this could be where his love of literature began. His lack of understanding of the Scriptures was not helped by Henry insisting on teaching Edmund points of doctrine and interpretation that were well beyond someone so young. It was all in the need to maintain and develop dedication to the same brand of Christianity that Henry followed; the only possible way. Of course, this entailed constant adverse references to the Papacy and to Catholicism in general.

Then a third major figure appeared in this introspective household; Miss Sarah Andrews (changed to Miss Marks in *Father and Son*) who was to be both housekeeper and a governess for Edmund. From his description, Miss Andrews sounds rather severe and quiet but, although Edmund reflects that she was reminiscent of a character in a Dickens novel, Sarah was kind-hearted and dutiful. She was not well educated, but her task as governess was made simple by Edmund's love of knowledge. Miss Andrews had undergone a religious conversion and she wholeheartedly believed in all that Henry said about Christianity, so perhaps he was the agent of her conversion, something which often produces a strong bond of 'teacher and student'? Miss Andrews' zeal as a convert was a lesser influence on Edmund than Henry's constant and weighty pronouncements, as can be deduced from Edmund's remark in *Father and Son*: 'On my own religious development she had no great influence. Any such guttering theological rushlight as Miss [Andrews] might dutifully exhibit faded for me in the blaze of my father's glaring beacon-lamp of faith.'

At this point in time Henry decided to leave London for St Marychurch, and made a prospecting trip to the village, which is now part of Torquay. While riding on horseback around the area he discovered a newly-built villa and, after praying for guidance, bought the property. This was Sandhurst and, even though it was barely completed and in need of decoration, the Gosse household moved to the new house. It meant that Edmund, like Henry (and myself), spent much of his boyhood near the coast, later tracing his love of the sea, and of seascapes, to this time. In *Father and Son*, Edmund describes Oddicombe, the nearest beach to St Marychurch, as being unspoilt and with only a path leading down to the water.

Oddicombe Beach today. (From Author's Collection).

I have visited Oddicombe many times and it is still possible to reach the shore by taking a steep path winding through the woods. Edmund's visits to Oddicombe were usually made with his father, as Henry frequently collected there, and it is not difficult to envisage father and son walking quickly down the path to start work and then trudging back up the cliff side with specimens and sea water. It was the time when Edmund still felt close to Henry emotionally, through the deep sadness of sharing their loss.

The path to Oddicombe Beach. (From Author's Collection).

Edmund admits to a compelling fantasy during these visits to the shore. In his imagination he would walk out over the sea, lie down on its surface and peer into the depths. He clearly didn't suffer my fear of having his head in the water; at least, not in his fantasy. Edmund, like many Victorians, was fascinated by this unknown realm and this extended to the Gosse's Cockney maid who tasted the sea water on her first visit to reassure herself it was salty. All this was, however, a diversion. Edmund found the winter of 1857 to be 'dismal' and the atmosphere in Sandhurst was not improved as the reviews of *Omphalos*, and letters about the book, started to come in. They were all negative and this would have been disappointing enough had Henry not been expecting praise; after all, he had untied the geological knot with his interpretation of prochronic existence. The mood was too much for Miss Andrews who often retreated to her room, which Edmund was not allowed to enter, so he spent most time in his father's company. They went for walks, but conversation was not like it had been earlier in London when they leaned over bridges and watched ducks and chatted. Now there was nothing but gloom and Edmund was affected, even describing himself as being very cantankerous and difficult. He also had catarrh.

There were meetings with fellow Christians, but they were not likely to involve conversation about the matters that were pre-occupying Henry. Reactions to *Omphalos* also meant that Henry was now cut off from the Establishment and from Christians outside his very small circle. In *Father and Son*, Edmund writes:

> My father, although half suffocated by the emotion of being lifted, as it were, on the great biological wave, never dreamed of letting go his clutch of the ancient tradition, but hung there, strained and buffeted. It is extraordinary that he – an "honest hodman of science" as [T. H.] Huxley once called him – should not have been content to allow others, whose horizons were wider than his could be, to pursue those purely intellectual surveys for which he had no species of aptitude. As a collector of facts and marshaller of observations, he had not a rival in that age; his very absence of imagination aided him in this work. But he was more an attorney than a philosopher, and he lacked that sublime humility which is the crown of genius. For, this obstinate persuasion that he alone knew the mind of God, that he alone could interpret the designs of the creator, what did it result from if not from a congenital lack of the highest modesty which replies "I do not know" even to the questions which Faith, with menacing finger, insists on having most positively answered?

A tough, but realistic, criticism and there is nothing here of Henry's great talent as a communicator of Natural History. Edmund recognises Henry's strong points as a scientist, but also quotes Huxley's patronising statement implying that Henry's contributions were far from major. Could they have been major if he wasn't imprisoned by his faith and felt he must write *Omphalos*? Who knows? As Darwin's theory was accepted widely by the scientific community and by the Establishment at the time *Father and Son* was published, there is no question of where Edmund's sympathies lay with regard to his father's conflict, expressed so obviously in *Omphalos*. But let's get back to St Marychurch.

The religious community of which Henry and Edmund were part was far removed from the sophisticated circles of society, and of the Learned Societies, in London. Their life at this time revolved around this small group and the collecting trips made to the shore. Edmund describes the members of the St Marychurch congregation of Brethren as 'pious rustics' and Henry almost immediately became their leader after the Gosses moved to Devon. He preached and celebrated the Breaking of Bread, maintaining his zealous approach even when few attended. Some ceremonies were performed on Oddicombe beach, often accompanied by jeering from irreverent spectators, but worship centred on their small chapel. Edmund writes of several members of this congregation. There was James Petherbridge who came to the chapel in a full smock and who prayed aloud for the Lord to support the local schoolteacher in her work (how reminiscent of my own experience at Torquay Grammar School Christian Union Prayer Meetings). Mr Petherbridge's jaw dropped into an expression of open-mouthed awe when Henry was preaching in full flow, so impressed was he with the delivery of the Word. Another regular was Richard Moxhay, younger than Mr Petherbridge, and always dressed in a suit of white corduroy. Both he and his wife were taciturn and this annoyed Henry; they 'never spoke unless they were spoken to.'

Of course, Miss Andrews was a member of the congregation and she developed a strong friendship with Mary Grace Hannaford (given the surname Burmington in *Father and Son*), one of three orphaned sisters who ran a china shop in St Marychurch. As Mary Grace was such a close friend of Miss Andrews, she also became a friend to Edmund. She was short and suffered from a deformed spine, but was of good nature and she was young, less than thirty when Edmund was nine. As Henry disliked calling on members of the congregation at home, this task was taken on with enthusiasm by Mary Grace and she often took Edmund along. He, too, felt his own nervousness in meeting people and found the Devonian accent difficult, but his main recollection was of all the different smells in the houses and cottages that they visited together. Edmund 'dreaded and loathed' these smells but admits to this being part of his neurotic nature. On occasions, it put Edmund off his food on return to Sandhurst and he was increasingly reluctant to take part in any of the visits, mirroring Henry's dislike of the exercise. One place provided an exception; the village of Barton, which was surrounded by countryside that Edmund found magical, even though Mary Grace would not allow him to venture into it as he was, in her view, too young. It is clear that Sandhurst was grander than the houses and cottages of other members of the congregation. Perhaps it was not just shyness, but also snobbery that made Henry decline to make visits, while being happy for Mary Grace, and Edmund, to do so? Did he also feel that seeing how others lived was good for the boy?

When they returned from visits, Henry asked Mary Grace and Edmund about the responses of those they had met and whether they had any new religious testimonies to offer. Henry encouraged Edmund to give his observations and the young boy found this paternal interest useful in maintaining his concentration during subsequent visits, never knowing what impressions his father may request once they had returned home. Although visits were necessary to ensure the unity of Henry's congregation, and (in my view) Edmund's continued indoctrination, the sanitary conditions in some cottages were so poor that, in time, Edmund was excused making the calls. Now, Mary Grace went inside the various homes and Edmund was left to watch wildlife and enjoy what the countryside had to offer.

In spring and summer of 1858 Henry returned to collecting on the sea shore, which Edmund acknowledged was where his father felt happiest:

Those pools were our mirrors, in which, reflected in the dark hyaline and framed by the sleek and shining fronds of oar-weed there used to appear the shapes of a middle-aged man and a funny little boy, equally eager, and, I almost find the presumption to say, equally well prepared for business.

Henry's spirits were improving as he recovered from the low point brought by the death of Emily and by the responses to *Omphalos*. Edmund felt happy too and it was the time leading up to *The Romance of Natural History*. There is affection in the writing in the quotation above, not just for scrabbling in rock pools but for making these excursions in Henry's company. This was still the period in which they were at their closest, but now there was less shared melancholy and Edmund was progressing on the path to salvation that his parents so desired. Edmund loved the untouched beauty of rock pools and he remarks that Henry would often wait before collecting just to admire the community of organisms presented. Writing in 1907, Edmund laments that these pristine shores changed dramatically in the fifty years since he was a boy and that Henry played a small part in this by encouraging collecting, about which he felt chagrin. What both Henry and Edmund would think of the seaside resort that was to develop around their collecting areas, and what became of that resort through the 1950s and 1960s when I grew up in Torbay, can only be speculated upon. I imagine it would have filled them with sadness.

Henry's methods of collecting were certainly destructive. As rocky shore organisms are often attached firmly to prevent them being washed away, it is not possible to remove just the organisms and then hope that they will somehow colonise when brought to an aquarium. To collect, Henry waded into deep pools, chiselled off fragments of rock to which animals and plants were attached and then placed the rock plus specimens into jars of sea water. The basket of collecting jars was usually very heavy and Henry carried it up the steep coastal tracks and back to Sandhurst.

There, the contents of each jar were spread into pans of clean sea water for observation. Although Edmund could never have Henry's accumulated and detailed knowledge of the marine flora and fauna, he was sharp-eyed and could easily spot organisms that Henry needed a lens to confirm. As a result, they were a partnership, and father and son must have enjoyed each other's company very much, both during, and after, collecting trips. It was the wonder of Natural History that conquered differences there may have been between them. The visits to the shore were certainly good for Edmund's health and he was less and less wrapped up in 'coats and comforters', an appearance that led some members of the chapel to comment on his sickliness. Both the cook and the housemaid at Sandhurst wondered whether he had long to live but, of course, the death of children was rather more commonplace then than it is now.

Life in St Marychurch at this time was not just a routine of studying, Brethren meetings, pastoral visits and collection trips along the shore. Edmund describes an exciting incident surrounding Miss Mary Flaw, the daughter of a retired Baptist minister and someone that he and Mary Grace visited in Barton. She always welcomed them warmly and supplied biscuits and Devonshire cream (then, as now, a very popular local produce). Miss Flaw was 'off the rails' and one never knew where her conversation was going to go next, something which Edmund loved. He found her 'brilliant and original.' She regularly attended the chapel and sat on the front bench, opposite Henry as the leader of proceedings and to the left of Mary Grace, Edmund and Miss Andrews who were on the right side of the same bench. When they rose from prayer, Miss Flaw would already be standing and singing an imaginary hymn. It was not unusual for her to rise up during one of Henry's sermons (which could last an hour), sing her hymn, collect her things and then walk out. In modern parlance, she seemed to be completely out of synch with reality and followed the procedure of her imagination, rather than that of the chapel. On one occasion, Edmund caught her eye as she gathered up her things and she darted across, grabbed him and the pair ran out of the chapel. This even caused Henry to stop his preaching and he led the congregation out to find Edmund and Miss Flaw sitting on the step of a butcher's shop. Edmund was recovered without a scene but it would seem that the experience clearly marked him.

He developed a fear that he was going to be abducted and this came back to him over and over again, especially at night. Edmund occasionally woke from dreams about being carried away and was so frightened that he uttered screams which brought his father and Miss Andrews rushing to him. Henry's response was to pray for exorcism and this was sometimes prolonged. The grim nature of it all was made worse on one occasion when a beetle crawled up from the foot of Edmund's bed and he uttered a scream when it reached as far as his face. Henry, in the middle of his prayer session, subsequently chastised Edmund because he had been disrespectful to God in making such an interruption to the communication:

"You, the child of a naturalist" he remarked in awesome tones, "*you* to pretend to feel terror at the advance of an insect?" It could be but a pretext, he declared, for avoiding the testimony of faith in prayer. "If your heart were fixed, if it panted after the Lord, it would take more than the movements of a beetle to make you disturb oral supplication at His footstool. Beware! For God is a jealous God and He consumes them in wrath who make a noise like a dog."

This was Henry as his most pious and apparently unfeeling, just as when he talked openly about Edmund's many misdemeanours at family prayers. This was done to keep him in the fold of believers, but it seems to have had the opposite effect. It's no wonder that Edmund turned against Henry's form of religion later in life for he had provided his son with almost endless ammunition for such a move.

After being kept from other children, even those from amongst the congregation at the chapel, the ten-year-old Edmund was now allowed to visit a boy of similar age, Benny, who lived in a large villa across the road. They enjoyed playing together in the gardens around the house, but their relationship was devoid of serious conversation, at least any that Edmund could recall later. Meanwhile, the isolated family life at Sandhurst was changing as the household began to receive visitors, among which were Charles Kingsley and Miss Wilkes, a young headmistress, who fascinated Edmund. She found Henry's instruction in Natural History to be important in revealing the wonders of God's Creation. It was the period when *The Romance of Natural History* was in gestation, and *Evenings at the Microscope* was published, and Henry was at his most energised. Miss Wilkes worked at the microscope, learned the Latin names of creatures and paid great attention to Henry's every word. When he remarked casually that women looked best in white stockings, she then wore stockings of that colour, rather than her preferred shade of deep violet. All very innocent, and Miss Wilkes certainly provided a breath of fresh air in both Henry's and Edmund's lives. However, the devotion of Miss Wilkes to Henry caused Miss Andrews to declare that the former was a 'minx' and the jealous governess, together with Mary Grace, prayed fervently that Henry would have his eyes opened to the fact.

As a young boy, Edmund was largely self-educated, although he was also taught some subjects by Miss Andrews and by his father. Henry now decided to teach Edmund Latin from a book used, years before, by Henry's father. Edmund had to learn pages of it while Henry studied or painted, and then show his knowledge of what he had learned. This had the unexpected effect of re-kindling Henry's love of Classics, something which had been very important to him during his early travels and at times when he felt isolated. The Latin verses that were learned in this way also had a profound effect on Edmund. Not the content, more the cadence: 'the amazing beauty that could exist in the sound of verses.'

Edmund grew rapidly as a ten-year-old and he no longer had the appearance that made some feel that he was not long for the world. This growth spurt brought with it the mental strength to overcome his hesitancy and fear of meeting people, and he started expressing his opinions more freely, opinions which up until then had formed in his mind but which he dared not utter. This was two years after the loss of his mother and both father and son were now able to be cheerful and even friendly. It's almost as though the pendulum of emotion had now overshot a little. Henry continued to work on *Actinologia Britannica* and Edmund expressed the closeness between the two by modelling himself on Henry in writing mini-monographs on creatures based on those he had seen during collecting trips, complete with imaginative paintings that unfortunately reflected his lack of talent as an artist. In so doing, he may have been looking for Henry's approval, and his father suggested that, instead of copying him, Edmund should 'go out into the garden or the shore and describe something new, in a new way.' Edmund thus continued as a mini-Henry, using a spare room as his study and writing and drawing on an old table. It became an obsession. Unlike Miss Andrews, Henry did not discourage this new interest, although he maintained his critical approach to Edmund's attempts at illustration.

It wasn't only Henry's work in Natural History and Science that Edmund copied, as he also tried to imitate Henry's religious side. The work on mini-monographs could not deflect from the main purpose of life in the Gosse household and Henry had concerns about Edmund's religious development and wanted him to be 'received into the community of the Brethren on the terms of an adult.' Their closeness at this time must have caused Henry to reflect on Emily's dying words and also on wanting to keep Edmund with him forever, with the Second Coming being imminent. Having one so young proposed to be a Saint did not go down well with all members of the Brethren chapel, but Henry overruled them. To become an adult member required an act of religious conversion, one which transformed the life of an individual to be a true believer. Nevertheless, Henry felt that as Edmund had been brought up in a family and household where faith ruled, his conversion was a steady, rather than a dramatic process. The majority of the congregation were of simple faith and obeyed the tenets that they were given, so there was confusion among them over this approach, as it was clearly not based on a definite time of conversion. Several members felt that their children should be accorded the same privilege as that to be given to Edmund, with the opposition coming mainly from the men in the congregation, women being more accommodating and wanting to support their leader's view. Indeed, many of the women elevated Edmund to be 'another Infant Samuel.' All this information was reported to Henry via Mary Grace after her visits to the believers, and the whole episode shows the darker side of Henry as a domineering dogmatist, albeit driven by love and fear.

In one of the Brethren meetings Henry pronounced that Edmund was to be admitted as an adult member of the congregation, able to take communion because he had been converted 'in still earlier infancy.' He declared that Brother Fawkes and Brother Bere, two of the main opponents of Henry's decision, should examine the case. This was such a clever move that the meeting broke up with warm agreement all round, and father and son returned to Sandhurst in high spirits. Edmund teased Henry by asking if, after baptism, he could call him 'beloved Brother', which thought must have appealed to a ten-year-old son and Henry met the question with good humour. Just as with Edmund's attempts to produce monographs, it was an example of a child eager to please his father.

Edmund was interviewed first by Mr Fawkes and Mr Bere

separately, and then by the two men together. He felt excited at the prospect, for it was a chance for him to impress, but he was also nervous. His first questioner was Mr Fawkes, who was uneasy and embarrassed about being a judge. Edmund took the lead and gave his testimony with such aplomb that Mr Fawkes was reduced to tears. Mr Bere represented more of a challenge as he used an interrogative approach, but Edmund also came though this interview well and the two elders returned, and then prayed together with Edmund. All the emotion of the occasion caused Edmund to weep and, exhausted, he was carried up to bed by Miss Andrews. The whole experience must have given Edmund yet more confidence in his abilities and he notes, on reflection, that this was the first time Mr Fawkes and Mr Bere had been in Sandhurst when it was fully decorated. They were impressed with the wallpaper in the drawing room, where the interviews took place. In *Father and Son*, Edmund is mocking here, albeit in a subtle way, but people often become diverted during a solemn occasion by something trivial. I certainly saw it at Winner Street Baptist Church and it's rather human.

On the Sunday following the meetings at Sandhurst, the congregation met to hear what Brothers Fawkes and Bere had to say. Henry asked them to give their views and both were effusive and positive. Edmund knew from the meetings that this would be the outcome, but it was nevertheless enjoyable to hear his saintliness described in front of the congregation. The verdict was a clear one: that Edmund should be admitted to the congregation as an adult believer. There was an enthusiastic response from those present, and some members later escorted Henry and Edmund back to Sandhurst in noisy celebration, to the bewilderment of onlookers. It would be wrong to describe the response as being hysterical, but many of us are familiar with the high emotion that is associated with key events in some branches of evangelical Christianity, and of other religions, of course. Edmund becoming a Saint was certainly a major event for the

St Marychurch Brethren.

In *Father and Son*, Edmund describes his baptism as 'the central event of my whole childhood', with everything leading to it, and from it. As baptisms were no longer conducted at Oddicombe Beach, and the St Marychurch Brethren did not have a pool in their room, services of baptism were conducted in a neighbouring large chapel. On these occasions, the different congregations mixed and chatted, and they were enjoyably social, as well as being highly-charged religious events. On 12 October 1859, Edmund was dressed in old clothes and with Henry, Miss Andrews, Mary Grace and a carpet bag containing a suit, set off by hansom cab for the chapel. Here, they were met with much excitement and were shown to their places on the front row. The chapel was usually poorly filled, but on this day it was packed, such was the spread of the news about the baptism of a ten-year-old. Others were to be baptised but, of course, they were all adults, so Edmund was the focus of attention, in which he revelled. In *Father and Son* he claimed that even 'worldly persons accustomed to life and to its curious and variegated experiences' would have been impressed by the spectacle.

If it was possible, the drama was made more compelling when a young woman, whose parents had forbidden her to be baptised, launched herself into the pool at the beginning of the service. This strange incident drew even more emotion from the believers gathered, but the next day Henry assured Edmund that she had not been baptised as at no time was her head under water. She was led away to an enclosed area resembling a tent and the service proper began. 'Mr S', the leader, announced a hymn and, while this was being sung, Edmund was taken by Miss Andrews and Mary Grace to the tent to prepare. The hymn singing stopped when Mr S was ready and this was a sign for Edmund to emerge from the tent and move to the pool. By now, all the congregation was silent and, with one hand on Edmund's chest and one on his back, Mr S pronounced: 'I baptize thee, my Brother, in the name of the Father and of the Son and of the Holy Ghost!', after which Edmund was tipped backwards to be fully immersed. He was then pulled up and Mr S made sure that he was safely delivered to Miss Andrews and Mary Grace, who hurried him to the tent. The silence was now broken by enthusiastic hymn singing. It was just like the two services of baptism that I had attended as a boy at Winner Street Baptist Church in Paignton, even the language seemingly almost identical. As I write, I can feel how it must have been to be part of the congregation in the Brethren chapel 150 years ago.

Henry was filled with joy at the result of the proceedings, showing rare signs of physical affection towards his saved and "adult" son. They were now both prepared for the Second Coming and Emily's dying wishes had been fulfilled. For Edmund, the aftermath brought a developing sense of independence and he felt able to share religious conversation with his father as a result. His status as the young convert also filled him with pride, so that he could be haughty and a little arrogant on occasions, even with the young friends with whom he was now associating.

Shortly after this most important event, the congregation moved from their old room above a stable to a custom-built chapel in the middle of St Marychurch village. They were expanding as Henry's fame as a preacher and leader spread, all this despite his shyness and difficulty in making contact with others. The congregation included the Saints and younger people who, of course, were interested in meeting each other, as well as in salvation. *Father and Son* contains two marvellous sentences about Henry's attitude to the behaviour of some of the young:

It was a very great distress to him that sometimes the young men and women who showed the most lively interest in Scripture, and who had apparently accepted the way of salvation with the fullest intelligence, were precisely those who seemed to struggle with least success against a temptation to unchastity. He put this down to the concentrated malignity of Satan, who directed his most poisoned darts against the fairest of the flock.

This type of distraction for the young people was not all. There were examples of drunkenness and 'all sorts of petty jealousy and scandal', perhaps to be expected in any community, especially a small one. These misdemeanours were detailed by Henry to Edmund and the build-up in concern about the whole business resulted in a sermon where the assembled congregation were scared by Henry's chastising and they were all told to fast. There was no familiar, friendly reception for the leader at the end of this service, and Edmund gives the impression that Henry stormed off in deliberate and heartfelt indignation. In Sandhurst, meals were replaced by bread and water, but Edmund did not record how long it continued, or to what extent the whole story of the fast was embellished in his narrative. This all took place early in 1860, when the writing of *The Romance of Natural History* was in full swing.

There was no prospect of Edmund joining the Chapel misfits and, as he modelled his actions on those of his father, he was viewed by Henry to be all that was proper in one of the saved. This was a heavy burden and Edmund became aware that his own religious pronouncements, which so pleased everyone else, did not fill him with the expected strong feelings of a Saint. Although saved, he wasn't swept up by the emotion of this state of being. Arguably, this may have been the beginning of Edmund's realisation that he was not of the same dogmatic Christian bent as his father, but he still showed all the outward signs expected of him. Edmund's baptism was indeed a changing point for him, although not in the way that Henry had intended. As time passed, Edmund found that strict adherence to the religious principles required of a Saint in the Brethren was becoming arduous.

In addition to reading *The Penny Cyclopaedia*, Edmund had always liked geography and maps, and imagined how distant

151

islands might look, just as he had wondered what was in the deep sea when making collecting trips to the shore. As Henry had visited some of the islands in the West Indies that interested Edmund, a source of first-hand information was at hand. In response to one of his son's enquiries, Henry went to his bookcase and pulled down a copy of *Tom Cringle's Log*, an adventure novel by Michael Scott that contained descriptions of the West Indies, and which Henry had probably enjoyed reading after his own travels. It had, as the frontispiece, an engraving of Bluefields Bay, close to where Henry had stayed in Jamaica and which had special meaning for him. Edmund describes the frontispiece as being of 'Blewfields, the great lonely house in a garden of Jamaican all-spice', so either the copy he read was a different edition, or his recall was typically somewhat vague, complete with the mis-spelling.

Perhaps as the result of some guilt, the book was kept at the top of the bookcase, where it was unlikely to be seen readily. It was a revelation to Edmund, with its strong language, and accounts of fights, mutinies and derring-do. It was an insight into a very different world to that of Sandhurst and the devout Brethren, in which Edmund had been wrapped. Now, Edmund's solitary walks to Barton and surrounding areas were changed by the hope of exciting adventures, although he still shied away from contact with almost everyone he encountered.

By this time, Edmund had been enrolled in a local school and walked there from Sandhurst, sometimes in the company of school friends. On one walk he met an elderly Irish gentleman, Mr Sheridan Knowles, and, overcoming his reticence, allowed himself to be drawn into conversation. After a time, Mr Knowles became a friend of sorts, as they met so frequently. He was a Baptist minister, but had previously been a well-known actor and dramatist and, to Edmund's delight, a published poet. His fame was such that he even received a mention in Bradshaw's *Descriptive Railway Hand-Book* of 1863 [3] as being a visitor to Great Malvern for the Water Cure. Having a wide knowledge of the theatre, Mr Knowles introduced Edmund to the works of Shakespeare, and recommended that the boys should study *The Merchant of Venice*. Edmund passed on this suggestion and the schoolmaster agreed; the boys enjoying reading aloud from a single volume of the play passed amongst them. The readings stopped abruptly one day and, although the cause of the stoppage was not known, Edmund believed that it was at Henry's request, as Henry did not read Shakespeare and had a disdain for the theatre. It seems that plays were acceptable for Baptists, but not for their close Christian relatives, the Brethren.

The religious side of Edmund's life was still ever present and while he mixed with the other boys, they were sometimes alienated by his asking whether they had been saved, again mimicking his father. Nevertheless, he joined in their games and they were awestruck by his knowledge of Geography. As Edmund was not worried about being on his own, he spent time at a horse pond near the school, making harbours and fortifications and imagining the pond to be some large ocean that might have appeared in *Tom Cringle's Log*. The local blacksmith, a member of the Brethren, saw Edmund at work on the muddy margin and told Henry about it. As Edmund reflected later, it was unusual behaviour for an adult who had been baptised in the faith. Another person who showed an interest in his constructions at the pond was Miss Brightwen, who sometimes came to Brethren meetings and was lodging in the area. They chatted about what he was doing and the conversation was clearly pleasing to both. There would be many more conversations when, in time, Miss Brightwen became the second Mrs P. H. Gosse.

The way in which Henry broached the subject of his forthcoming marriage is described touchingly by Edmund in

Father and Son:

> I slept in a little bed in a corner of the room, and my Father in the ancestral four-poster nearer the door. Very early one bright September morning at the close of my eleventh year, my Father called me over to him. I climbed up, and was snugly wrapped in the coverlid; and then we held a momentous conversation. It began abruptly by his asking me whether I should like a new mamma. I was never a sentimentalist, and I therefore answered, cannily, that that would depend on who she was. He parried this, and announced that, anyway, a new mamma was coming; I was sure to like her.

After further questions, Henry revealed that it was Miss Brightwen who was to become Edmund's stepmother and, almost as a reflex, the boy asked if she had 'taken up her cross in baptism.' A somewhat flurried Henry replied that she had been brought up in 'the so-called Church of England', and had thus already been baptised as a baby. As their conversation proceeded, both agreed that with their joint prayers, and by both Henry and Edmund presenting their views on the matter, she would become converted and wish to be baptised as an adult and thus become a Saint. It was a natural step, as she already attended meetings of the Brethren.

Given that Eliza Brightwen's choice of husband did not have the support of her family, and knowing Henry's innate shyness, it is not beyond likelihood that she did the initial chasing. Henry was looked up to by his community and, styling himself P. H. Gosse FRS, was recognisable as someone of distinction. Notwithstanding, their relationship was based on mutual affection and respect. Henry and Eliza married in December 1860 and came back to Sandhurst, with Edmund moving to a room of his own. It was then with some pride that Henry was delighted to tell the congregation that his new bride was to be baptised.

Just as during their meetings at the pond, Edmund and Eliza

enjoyed each other's company and he appreciated her refinement and interest in the arts. He also felt that she wasn't by nature, inclined to be as dogmatic in her beliefs as his father. To be sure, she could fret from time to time, and there may have been occasions when she found bowing to Henry's wishes rather trying, but it was a harmonious expanded family. Eliza certainly had different views to Sarah Andrews on the subject of caring for Edmund. Whereas Sarah wrapped him up in clothes or bedclothes, Eliza had a freer approach and encouraged him to enjoy fresh air. Henry was clearly occupied with Eliza, and as a result Edmund was also allowed a freedom that he had not had before and this led to him losing some of the dogma that he was brought up to believe as beyond question. Although still just as avid in his religious beliefs and his prayers, Henry maintained the optimistic and outward-looking frame of mind that showed in the two volumes of *The Romance of Natural History*. Edmund describes Henry as being able 'to clothe the darkness of the world with at least a mist of rose-colour'; an interesting comment given the content of *The Romance* and the almost playful Preface to the *First Series*.

Given his new sense of freedom, Edmund now spent time with boys who were from religious 'but not fanatical' families. There was also a relaxation in what he was permitted to read. Eliza brought with her a small library of books, including the poems of Walter Scott, which Henry read aloud to Eliza, such was his good mood. Edmund's developing love of poetry and other literature was stimulated by these readings, so Eliza suggested to Henry that the boy could read some of Scott's novels but, unfortunately, permission was not forthcoming, although Edmund was allowed to read Dickens, so that was a new opening. It wasn't just in literature that Eliza brought a fresh approach to life at Sandhurst, as her interest in painting meant that Edmund and Henry were encouraged to visit a local room where a work by Holman Hunt was on show. They all admired the colours and the details, as

Holman Hunt's technique had similarities to that used by Henry, and in turn Edmund, in painting the organisms of the sea shore. It was at this show that Edmund's interest in the Pre-Raphaelites was born, and this school of painters and poets was to play an important part in his future career and private life. The awakening of Edmund's love of art and literature coincided with the loosening of his ties to the limited religious views of the Brethren and, although the family still prayed together for guidance, Edmund began to feel adolescent rebellion against the religious straitjacket.

Meanwhile, Eliza's attempts to encourage Henry to attend meetings in London, to read papers at the Royal Society, to meet with fellow Zoologists, and to conduct field courses were not successful. He may have been concerned at the reception he would get after the hostile responses towards *Omphalos*, but it meant that Henry was retreating into his social shell once more. It was the beginning of the slide into the years when he wrote little, despite maintaining an active correspondence on scientific matters. This disappointed Eliza as she recognised how much he had to offer and was always ready to champion Henry's work. It was the start of Henry and Eliza becoming the 'Two Happy Old Fogies' described so well by Ann Thwaite in *Glimpses of the Wonderful*. The emotional pendulum was now swinging back to its normal position after the relative exuberance resulting from Henry's recovery from Emily's bereavement and from the reactions to *Omphalos*. Although Edmund respected, loved, and admired his father, he now knew him to fallible, and *Father and Son* details events that furthered Edmund's independence of mind. It was becoming clear that the wishes of both Emily and Henry that Edmund should be a devout Saint were not likely to be fulfilled.

Edmund was now attending a boarding school for the sons of evangelicals, returning home at weekends. It was not as rigorously religious as Henry believed it to be, but Edmund had no wish to tell his father this. Following Henry's instructions, Edmund didn't share a dormitory at the school with other boys of his age, but roomed with two sons of a Brethren acquaintance instead. They were older than Edmund, so it was not a comfortable arrangement for him, or them, and it couldn't have helped his feeling of being locked in to a very limited world.

It wasn't just a routine of school and the Brethren chapel though. On one occasion, Edmund travelled with Henry to London to attend a conference for evangelicals. It was most likely to have been in 1864, when Edmund was 15 years old and they stayed in a dingy hotel off The Strand. Edmund was left to his own devices during breaks when Henry went to the British Museum or the Royal Society, to pursue his research, but there is no mention in *Father and Son* of Eliza being with them. Yet she must have been there, as she and Henry did not spend a day apart until 1866, according to her comments in Appendix I of *The Naturalist of the Sea-Shore*. Perhaps it's another case of Edmund embellishing the truth to some extent?

Edmund could not remember any of the detail of the 'interminable ritual of prayers, hymns and addresses' at the conference, but he certainly remembered a comment from one delegate, who denounced Shakespeare and imagined that he was suffering in Hell. This denunciation was likely to have been occasioned by the Shakespeare tercentenary celebrations, which were taking place in Stratford. The outburst horrified him and, when they returned to the hotel for lunch, he expected Henry to agree with the speaker, but he did not. Instead, he argued that it was not possible to know if Shakespeare was in Hell and, anyway, so little was known of his life that 'we cannot know that Shakespeare did not accept the atonement of Christ in simple faith before he came to die.' On hearing this, Edmund wrote: 'The concession will today seem meagre to gay and worldly spirits, but words cannot express how comfortable it was to me. I gazed at my Father with loving eyes across the cheese and celery, and if the waiter had not been present I believe I might have hugged him in my arms.' It shows their emotional closeness and how thrilled Edmund was by this slight shift from Henry's usual position. He may have pondered on this whilst on their journey back to St Marychurch.

At times when he was ill during the week, and thus unable to go away to school, Edmund stayed at Sandhurst and enjoyed the attentions of Eliza. He then had time to read, away from the less compelling studies he would otherwise have to endure. Eliza listened to Edmund reading aloud but there was one occasion when he unknowingly overstepped a mark of decency and she asked him for the book, closed it and placed it under her needlework. Edmund later saw how limited his life was at that point and later recalled:

My prayers became less frigid and mechanical; I no longer avoided as far as possible the contemplation of religious ideas; I began to search the Scriptures for myself with interest and sympathy, if scarcely with ardour. I began to perceive, *without animosity* [author's italics], the strange narrowness of my Father's system, which seemed to take into consideration only a selected circle of persons, a group of disciples peculiarly illuminated, and to have no message whatever for the wider Christian community ... Taking for granted, as he did, the absolute integrity of the Scriptures, and applying to them his trained scientific spirit, he contrived to stifle, with a deplorable success, alike the function of the imagination, the sense of moral justice, and *his own deep and instinctive tenderness of heart* [author's italics].

So, Edmund did not feel angry about having to live in the world according to Henry and was saddened by the effect of rigid religious belief on Henry's otherwise kind and understanding nature. That argues against the idea that *Father and Son* was written as a form of revenge against Henry for providing a difficult, yet warm, childhood, which begs the question, *why* did Edmund write it? Did he speculate that it was going to be the book that made him famous, because it centred on the contrasting religious and secular sensibilities of the time?

A developing sense of his religious isolation made Edmund interested in attending other churches, like the local parish church or a Roman Catholic service, but this was, inevitably, out of the question. Acknowledging again that Henry treated him with indulgence and affection, Edmund knew that he could not embarrass his father by sneaking in to services where he would surely be seen. However, he could be a little more independent when away at school, not in visiting churches *per se*, but in exploring his own religious standpoint. Edmund recalls an occasion when he was reading alone on a beautiful evening and, as he looked out across the school grounds, it was so perfect that he was ready to anticipate the End and asked that God should take him then and there. Nothing happened. That was a pivotal moment, for he realised from that point on that his religious views would never be reconciled with those of his father.

Edmund's Epilogue in Father and Son

In the Epilogue of *Father and Son*, Edmund moves away from descriptions of his life as a boy to consider 'the unique and noble figure of the Father.' Inevitably, it is largely about the growing distance between the two men.

At 17, Edmund was living in London and had begun working in the British Museum, so Henry was left to his settled 'fogey'-like existence with Eliza. At first, he kept up a vigorous correspondence with Edmund, full of enquiries about conduct and contacts. As would be expected of any young person exploring their own ideas and seeking independence in so many ways, Edmund found this stifling. Even though the stream of letters was tempered by chatty notes from Eliza, it was not easy to answer all the questions posed by his father. Sometimes he replied in exactly the way Henry would have wished, at other times he would ignore the bombardment, or even request not to have such relentless enquiry. For his part, Henry would try to accommodate Edmund's wishes, yet he always returned to interrogation. He was especially interested in new friends who were 'agreeable company', but not fellow believers in the truth as understood by the Brethren. Henry always carried the anxiety that Edmund might drift away from absolute belief and therefore not be ready for the imminent return of Christ.

To help maintain the young man on the only path to salvation, Henry had presented Edmund with the four volumes of Dean Alford's edition of the Greek New Testament, bound in Morocco leather covers. He was exhorted to translate some text each day before he left for work but, of course, he didn't comply. This pricked Edmund's conscience, as he knew that the omission would hurt his father, but he had become bored with re-reading lines which were so familiar to him. His approach was in stark contrast to Henry's, for whom pondering over the meanings of words and sections of text in The Bible was an essential daily discipline, first encouraged by his mother when he was young. Another reason for Edmund's lack of enthusiasm for studying his handsome copies of the New Testament was his discovery of the many other works of literature which were now available to him, providing new enjoyment and stimulus.

We don't know to what extent it was intentional, but Edmund revealed in his letters to his father that he was not following the path that was proscribed and was deemed essential. Henry was hurt by this and he also worried about the possibilities for backsliding that a young man faced in London. They were referred to constantly as 'pitfalls', but Edmund had now developed a strong dislike of his father's position and the correspondence became less significant to him. As the following extract shows, Henry was becoming less persistent:

As time went on, the peculiar strain of inquisition was relaxed, and I endured fewer and fewer of the torments of religious correspondence.

Nothing abides in one tense projection, and my Father, resolute as he was, had other preoccupations. His orchids, his microscope, his physiological researches, his interpretation of prophecy, filled up the hours of his active and strenuous life, and, out of his sight, I became not indeed out of his mind, but no longer ceaselessly in the painful foreground of it. Yet, although the reiteration of his anxiety might weary him a little as it had wearied me well nigh to groans of despair, there was not the slightest change in his real attitude towards the subject or towards me.

Edmund then re-iterates that, although Henry had a deep Christian belief, he was also a rationalist and was not prone to flights of imagination in expecting to see miracles or such like. Henry was also scathing of those that made claims that had little basis other than fantasy. It was another reason for his profound opposition to mystical religious sects and those denominations such as Roman Catholicism, often despised by Nonconformists, which require evidence of miracles as a pre-requisite for sainthood and believe in transubstantiation during Communion.

Visits made by Edmund to St Marychurch were marked by mental sparring between father and son. Henry had mostly been in the company of the simple folk in the Brethren congregation and they did not engage in intellectual debate, so Edmund's arrival was welcomed as much for the chance to pursue argument, as for the more obvious reasons of contact between loved ones. Henry habitually 'won' these encounters, not by the quality of his debating, but by the constant reference to the powers of God and of righteousness. The one-sided encounters gave Henry great pleasure and he would become emotional with the thought that, once more, his religious beliefs had produced arguments that could not be countered. It was not a very pleasant characteristic and he was incapable of seeing what folly this was, in just the same way as he had been baffled by the reaction to *Omphalos*.

Needing a sense of victory in argument indicates that Henry must surely have experienced some doubts about his beliefs. Yet, these were contained and remained a private matter, for he stolidly maintained the appearance of complete commitment, as Edmund shows in this passage:

> I earnestly desire that no trace of that absurd self-pity which is apt to taint recollections of this nature should give falsity to mine. My Father, let me say once more, had other interests than those of his religion. In particular, at this time, he took to painting in water-colours in the open air, and he resumed the assiduous study of botany. He was no fanatical monomaniac. Nevertheless, there was, in everything he did and said, the central purpose present. He acknowledged it plainly; "with me", he confessed, "every question assumes a Divine standpoint and is not adequately answered in the judgement-seat of Christ is not kept in sight."

The Epilogue of *Father and Son* closes with a powerful attack on Henry's position. Although the onslaught of religious dogma could be deflected by Eliza's intervention (and Edmund clearly remained very fond of his stepmother, who died before the publication of *Father and Son*) it was Henry's never-ending quest to make sure that Edmund was a believer. One question was repeated often: was Edmund 'walking closely with God?' Like many profound believers, of whatever faith, Henry's personal approach to achieving salvation was at the expense of the pleasantries of wide-ranging human contact. For Henry, his beliefs were very serious indeed, although he saw himself as a mere servant of God. The final pages of the Epilogue quote from a letter from Henry that demonstrates just how divided the father and son had become and, as Edmund points out, there could be no chance of a compromise. It was sent immediately after a visit by Edmund to Torquay, when the son made an emotional attempt to defend his position and 'begged to be left alone':

> When your sainted Mother died, she not only tenderly committed you to God, but left you also as a solemn charge to me, to bring you

up in the nurture and admonition of the Lord. That responsibility I have sought constantly to keep before me: I can truly aver that it *has* been ever before me – in my choice of a housekeeper, in my choice of a school, in my ordering of your holidays, in my choice of a second wife, in my choice of an occupation for you, in my choice of a residence for you; and in multitudes of lesser things – I have sought to act for you, not in the light of this present world, but with a view to Eternity.

Before your childhood was past, there seemed God's manifest blessing on our care; for you seemed truly converted to Him; you confessed, in solemn baptism, that you had died and had been raised with Christ; and you were received with joy into the bosom of the Church of God, as one alive from the dead.

All this filled my heart with thankfulness and joy, whenever I thought of you: - how could it do otherwise? And when I left you in London, on that dreary winter evening, my heart, full of sorrowing love, found its refuge and its resource in this thought, – that you were one of the lambs of Christ's flock; sealed with the Holy Spirit as His; renewed in heart to holiness, in the image of God.

For a while, all appeared to go on fairly well: we yearned, indeed, to discover more of heart in your allusions to religious matters, but your expressions towards us were filial and affectionate; your conduct, so far as we could see, was moral and becoming; you mingled with the people of God, spoke of occasional delight and profit in His ordinances; and employed your talents in service to Him.

But of late, and specially during the past year, there has become manifest a rapid progress towards evil. (I must beg you here to pause, and again look to God for grace to weigh what I am about to say; or else wrath will rise).

When you came to us in the summer, the heavy blow fell full upon me; and I discovered how very far you had departed from God. It was not that you had yielded to the strong tide of youthful blood, and had fallen a victim to fleshly lusts; in that case, however sad, your enlightened conscience would have spoken loudly, and you would have found your way back to the blood which cleanseth us from all sin, to humble confession and self-abasement, to forgiveness and to recommunion with God. It was not this; it was worse. It was that horrid, insidious infidelity, which had already worked in your mind and heart with terrible energy. Far worse, I say, because this was sapping the very foundations of faith, on which all true godliness, all real religion, must rest.

Nothing seemed left to which I could appeal. We had, I found, no common ground. The Holy Scriptures had no longer any authority: you had taught yourself to evade their inspiration. Any particular Oracle of God which pressed you, you could easily explain away; even the very character of God you weighed in your balance of fallen reason, and fashioned it accordingly. You were thus sailing down the rapid tide of time towards Eternity, without a single authoritative guide (having cast your chart overboard), except what you might fashion and forge on your own anvil, – except what you might *guess*, in fact.

Do not think I am speaking in passion, and using unwarrantable strength of words. If the written Word is not absolutely authoritative, what do we know of God? What more then can we infer, that is, guess, – as the thoughtful heathens guessed, – Plato, Socrates, Cicero, – from dim and mute surrounding phenomena? What do we know of Eternity? Of our relations to God? Especially of the relations of a *sinner* to God? What of reconciliation? What of the capital question – How can a God of perfect spotless rectitude deal with me, a corrupt sinner, who have trampled on those of His laws which were even written on my conscience? ...

This dreadful conduct of yours I had intended, after much prayer, to pass by in entire silence; but your apparently sincere inquiries after the cause of my sorrow have led me to go to the root of the matter, and I could not stop short of the development contained in this letter. It is with pain, not in anger, that I send it; hoping that you may be induced to review the whole course, of which this is only a stage, before God. If this grace were granted to you, oh! how joyfully should I bury all the past, and again have sweet and tender fellowship with my beloved Son, as of old.

It is easy to see in this letter how Henry's deep religious beliefs caused great pain, both for the father and for the son, and it shows so clearly the result of having differing views on something so profoundly serious to one party. Reading the letter, it is difficult not to feel an awful sadness and waste. Faith that was so supportive to one of the two (although generating anxiety) was driving a wedge between them, and their close emotional relationship was strained. How good that both Nellie and Eliza were there to ensure that some bridges remained in place.

Edmund must have kept the letter, or a summary of its contents, for fifty years, such was his hurt. In spite of this, the first biography has the description of the happy family day out at Goodrington and that's the way I want to remember them at the end. *The Naturalist of the Sea-Shore: The Life of Philip Henry Gosse* [4] closes with the touching scene of a carriage drive along the sea front at Torquay in which Edmund and Henry went to Cockington village. They would have passed the house where Henry's friend Charles Kingsley – author of *The Water-Babies, A Fairy Tale for a Land Baby*, had lived in 1854, and which is now part of the Livermead House Hotel – and on down Cockington Lane and under the bridge taking the railway line to Paignton. It was a beautiful afternoon and Edmund's description of part of the return journey, as they proceeded along Cockington Lane on the way back to Sandhurst is most poignant:

My father, with the pathetic look in his eyes, the mortal pallor on his cheeks, scarcely spoke, and seemed to observe nothing. But, as we turned to drive back down a steep lane of overhanging branches, the pale vista of the sea burst upon us, silvery blue in the yellow light of afternoon. Something in the beauty of the scene raised the sunken brain, and with a little of the old declamatory animation in head and hand, he began to recite the well-known passage in the fourth book of *Paradise Lost* – "Now came still evening on, and twilight grey – Had in her sober livery all things clad." He pursued the quotation through three or four lines, and then, in the middle of a sentence, the music broke, his head fell once more upon his breast, and for him the splendid memory, the self-sustaining intellect which had guided the body so long, were to be its companions on earth no more.

Cockington Lane today, looking towards the seafront and under the railway bridge; the route of the last carriage drive taken by Henry and Edmund.
(From Author's Collection).

This was in July 1888 and it was the last drive out that Henry took. The illness had immobilised him, but there was little pain and he died on 23 August 1888, being buried on 27 August in un-consecrated ground in Torquay Cemetery. Eliza, who lived to be 87, was buried in the same grave on 18 October 1900, with old Mrs Gosse buried nearby. Little did I know when growing up that this great Natural Historian lay such a short distance from Torquay Boys' Grammar School and its small-scale aquaria. The gravestone is still there, albeit fallen at an angle, and it is somewhat ironic that the Torquay Crematorium is in the same cemetery. Both my Mum and Dad were cremated there, but nothing marks the fact.

The grave of Philip Henry Gosse and Eliza Gosse in un-consecrated ground in Torquay Cemetery. (From Author's Collection).

Learning more about Edmund

Having encountered Edmund's view of Henry as a wonderful Natural Historian and illustrator; a rigid believer in the literal truth of The Bible; a Creationist; and a difficult, but loving father, it is time to discover more from this primary source of information on Henry's life and work.

Many years passed between Edmund's arrival in London and the publication of this second biography of Henry, combined, as it was, with the autobiography of Edmund's childhood. These years in London coloured his view of the events he described in the book. It is fortunate that, before writing *Glimpses of the Wonderful*, Ann Thwaite wrote *Edmund Gosse: A Literary Landscape*, [5] a comprehensive and scholarly work. It gives further insights into his early days, the relationship with Henry, and also of Edmund's subsequent great success as a member of the Establishment and Knight of the Realm.

Just as Philip Henry Gosse was probably known as Henry, it appears that Edmund William Gosse was called Willy by his parents, at least as a boy. There was obvious affection between father, mother and son and some of the letters quoted in Ann Thwaite's biography show much tenderness. Edmund's birth had not been easy (the equivalent of a modern forceps delivery) and he took some time to show clear signs of life but, after this traumatic start, he was quickly settled into a routine and Emily announced happily that he was given to the Lord. It was hoped that Hannah Gosse, who was living with them, would share in the mood and enjoy being a grandmother but, if this was her reaction, it did not unfreeze the chill between her and Emily, clearly based on wanting Henry's attentions all for herself. In the end, old Mrs Gosse left as their housekeeper and Kate Jones arrived as a domestic servant.

As mementoes of his son's early years, Henry made outlines of Edmund's right hand; his length from head to foot was recorded at intervals, and great pride was taken in watching his first steps. When Emily had to leave to nurse a dying aunt, Henry and Kate shared the responsibility of looking after Edmund, and one would conjecture that Kate took over when he became too demanding. Emily's diary entries reveal that she was anxious to be a good mother and, typically, was keen also that Kate should be converted. Another concern was financial and the threat of debts after their investment in the Cornish tin mine ran into difficulties.

When Henry was away, Edmund, as a young child, dictated letters for his father to Emily, who acted as amanuensis. Sometimes, dried flowers were placed in the envelope, as Edmund wanted to include tokens of his affection and the letters were usually effusive, telling Henry that he longed to see him again, to share kisses and go for walks. They enjoyed each other's company and it remained a happy and warm household, albeit with its strict and fearful religious foundation. This happiness was devastated by the onset of Emily's illness and her subsequent death; a key event in the lives of both father and son. After Emily died, Henry's feelings for Edmund were unsurprisingly reinforced and his strong paternal emotions were expressed in his correspondence. It seems characteristic that he was more comfortable expressing strong emotions by letter, rather than in person.

After the two Gosses moved to St Marychurch, Edmund wrote his own letters to Henry when he was away lecturing. These were typically childish in having love expressed with hyperbole and with dots to represent 'Willy kisses'. Although Edmund was able to express his feelings openly, there was always the pressure to be good and Ann Thwaite cites a letter from Sarah Andrews to Henry after a day when Edmund had lost his temper:

> ... saying things in passion which might have made much mischief between the maids and myself, but thank the Lord he has given us all much peace and has not allowed Satan to have power.

A child losing their temper and firing off at all and sundry is quite normal but Edmund's behaviour was reported as having been under the influence of Satan. This need for intense religious interpretations of even minor events takes me back to the time when a fellow student at Reading thought that I was the closest they had come to the Devil.

We read in *Edmund Gosse: A Literary Landscape* how Edmund acquired his first position in London, and Henry certainly worked his connections to make it happen. This contrasts with Henry's activities on his own behalf, yet he had, of course, been recommended to both Van Voorst and SPCK by Thomas Bell at the start of his career as a writer and he appreciated what needed to be done. Henry was keen that Edmund should take a post in the Civil Service, but entry at the time was not possible without the support and influence of patronage. Perhaps the most important of Henry's contacts was Charles Kingsley, for the two men reconciled after their conflict over the disputed passages in *Omphalos*. Kingsley was now Regius Professor of Modern History at Cambridge and 'went to enormous trouble for the son of his old companion.' This included contacting a distant relation by marriage, Theodore Walrond, one of the Civil Service Examiners, and Kingsley was also prepared to write to the Lord Chancellor. He arranged a meeting with Sir Anthony Panizzi, the Librarian of the British Museum, so Edmund's advance was thus not to be the result of Divine support alone.

On the day of the meeting with Sir Anthony, Henry and Edmund said their morning prayers and set off from Sandhurst, travelling First Class on the train to London, very expensive at the time, but always preferred by Henry. Was this another indication that he was a tad snobbish, or did it mean that he preferred his own thoughts during journeys, with the added bonus of being able to proselytise among those of elevated status? Henry must have been an uncomfortable travelling companion on occasions, as an elderly gentleman found when entering their carriage at Exeter. There was almost immediately an enquiry from Henry on whether their fellow traveller was a true believer. 'The answer was curt. The elderly gentleman withdrew to his corner of the carriage, buried himself in a book and took no further notice of them.' I think I know how he must have felt.

Edmund was intimidated on first meeting Panizzi and felt unsure about the path ahead, returning with Henry to Torquay with the advice that he should further his knowledge of languages. In the final phase of his school life, Edmund did indeed advance his language skills and he claimed to speak English and German, to write French and to read Greek, Latin and Italian. After more pulling of strings by Kingsley with leading members of the Establishment, including a lady who was 'not only an old friend of the Speaker of the House of Commons but also a great admirer of P. H. Gosse's books', a position was secured in the Library of the British Museum.

In London, Edmund took lodgings with an old friend of Henry's who was of similar religious persuasion and so began independent life. Working within the Civil Service, latterly at the Board of Trade, was not enjoyable and, to compensate, Edmund continued to write poetry and to make many further contacts in the literary world, both in England and, increasingly, in Scandinavia. He was on friendly terms with some of the Pre-Raphaelites and became well known in the best circles. It was through the Pre-Raphaelites that he met the artist Ellen [Nellie] Epps, who had links with the Brotherhood, and they were married in 1875, having three children by 1881.

The lessons of Kingsley's patronage, which resulted in his first appointment, had clearly been learned well and Edmund gathered influential backers for his attempt to be the first Clark Lecturer at Trinity College Cambridge. Among these were Matthew Arnold, Robert Browning, Alfred Tennyson and Sidney Colvin, a Fellow of Trinity. Despite this support, Edmund was not successful and the post went to Leslie Stephen, a Cambridge insider, and father of Virginia Woolf and Vanessa Bell, by one vote. Although well-connected, Edmund was not held universally in high regard and this may have influenced the panel as much as their choice of one of their own. Then, as now, it was not only about networking, but the advantage of being an insider.

After visiting America on a successful lecture tour, which included offers of academic posts, Edmund was very pleased to receive a letter from the Master of Trinity to say that Stephen had resigned the Clark Lectureship and that it had been agreed unanimously that the post should be offered to Edmund, for two years, commencing 1 October 1884. Twenty lectures were to be given in each year and Edmund based the first series of lectures on those he had given during his visit to America, and which had been received enthusiastically. He was pleased with the Clark Lectures and these were published as a book by Cambridge University Press in 1885. Just as the death of Emily was a pivotal time in Edmund's life, so was the publication of *From Shakespeare to Pope: an enquiry into the causes and phenomena of the rise of classical poetry in England.* [6] It was attacked for the many errors which it contained, and Edmund's knowledge of the history of literature was called into question. The leading critic was John Churton Collins, who held the Merton Chair of English Language and Literature at Oxford. He was perhaps disdainful as he had a university education and much experience as a teacher, so felt Edmund, who had neither, was a dilettante. Collins attacked many aspects of Edmund's book, probably quite rightly, but concluded that 'it illustrates comprehensively the manner in which English literature should not be taught.' It was all typical of the cruel taunting that can affect some academics, and Edmund received blow after blow in the ensuing discussions. It was well known that he was prone to inaccuracies, but his status was now threatened and he had periods of depression as a result. This context should be remembered when reading *Father and Son.*

Ann Thwaite was unable to find any correspondence between Edmund and Henry during this difficult time for the former. She suggests that Henry would have been annoyed by the errors in *From Shakespeare to Pope* if he had known about them, having always stressed to Edmund the importance of accuracy. The criticism and attacks had died down when Edmund and family visited Paignton in September 1887, where they had such a happy time with Henry at Goodrington. We cannot know what conversation on the controversy passed between father and son on that day, or whether Henry knew much about it. If there were more general frictions with Edmund, there seem to have been none with Nellie, who was much loved by Henry and Eliza. Their relationship was warm and friendly and, when Henry became very ill, Nellie joined Eliza in nursing him, leaving Edmund and the children in London where Edmund was part of the artistic élite and continued to meet with many of the leading figures of the day. But then came the visit to St Marychurch, and the last carriage ride with Henry to Cockington, who was now dying, although still fighting against it and perhaps still hoping for the imminent Second Coming as a much better alternative to death.

As would be expected, Henry's death brought emotional release for Edmund, and, especially for a part of his character and identity that would have appalled Henry, had he known. Edmund had a number of intimate male friends, including the sculptor Hamo Thornycroft. It is clear that these close relationships meant a great deal to him and his awareness of growing homosexual attractions may have further distanced him from Henry, who could never have condoned this preference. Was the discovery of his bisexuality another reason for Edmund to feel hostile towards Henry while growing up? Was it as significant as religion in driving an emotional wedge between them, expressed so clearly in *Father and Son*? We cannot know, nor can we know whether Henry's earnest pleas that Edmund should chose his London friends carefully and avoid 'pitfalls' were based on a fear that he was mixing with those thought to be homosexual (although this was unlikely to be admitted openly in Victorian society). Edmund was certainly very fond of Nellie and the children and, even when he was with Hamo and others, he wrote her letters expressing how much he missed her. Of course, Nellie knew about Edmund's sexual preferences, and it is another reason why she was keen to maintain the warm relationship with Henry and Eliza. Her bridge-building was to the benefit of all.

Henry left an estate of more than £16,000 and, after a gift of £1,000 to Edmund, the remainder was bequeathed to Eliza. The guilt that Edmund felt about his relationship with his father was relieved by work on the first biography and Eliza, of course, was very interested in all that was written, often to Edmund's consternation. Her own view of her time with Henry formed an

Appendix to the biography and this is covered in the following section of this book. After publication of *The Naturalist of the Sea-Shore: The Life of Philip Henry Gosse*, Edmund returned to his interest in literature and his professional and social circle but, inevitably, had doubts about his own ability, turning 'more and more to the consolations of the world, to the pleasures of talk and power.' Unlike *From Shakespeare to Pope*, the biography was well-received and several of Edmund's friends encouraged him to put more of himself into an autobiography, a seed which grew over the next twenty-five years into *Father and Son*.

Edmund William Gosse, age 37, painted by John Singer Sargent.
(With permission from the National Portrait Gallery).

Father and Son, still regarded as Edmund's best work, took well over a year to write and whilst it was published anonymously, it was very obvious that Henry and Edmund were the subjects, even with the changing of names that Edmund felt necessary. Eliza, the guardian of Henry's reputation, had died in 1900 and Edmund should have had no concern about offending his step-mother when writing the second, autobiographical book. However, the views of the relationship expressed in *Father and Son* must be seen against comments about the accuracy of Edmund's previous work and on his need to produce a masterpiece to maintain his position as a leading man of letters and influence. Mindful of his social position, this motive may have been of greater significance to him than any other. Edmund Gosse was awarded both a knighthood and the Legion d'Honneur in 1925, eighteen years after *Father and Son* was published.

Sir Edmund William Gosse (left) age 78, with Thomas Hardy.
(With permission from the National Portrait Gallery).

Having considered Edmund's account of being raised by Henry Gosse, we know more about his attitude to his father and how this may have been affected by his independent life. There are two other important sources of information on Henry. Firstly, that of Eliza and second, that of the close family of William Pengelly FRS, a friend from Torquay during Henry's outgoing phase of the later 1850s and early 1860s; the time of *The Romance of Natural History*.

Eliza Gosse's view of Henry

We know from *Father and Son* that Edmund appreciated the warmth and humanity of his stepmother, and found her notes in letters to be a counterpoint to Henry's stern enquiries during the early days of his independence in London. So what was Eliza's view of Henry? Her account in Appendix I of *The Naturalist of the Sea-Shore* [4] gives us the answer. It was written two years after Henry died and is respectful and untainted by religious warring. As Eliza shared Henry's views, she writes without prickliness and provides a parallel commentary to Edmund's two biographies.

Eliza's account begins by describing her first acquaintance with Henry during a visit to Torquay with her sister. They lodged at the cottage of a religious couple, Mr and Mrs Curtis, and met Leonard Strong who had just returned from Torquay Cemetery where he was present at the burial of Hannah Gosse, whom he identified as 'Mr Gosse's mother.' Eliza then enquired as to whether this was Mr Gosse the well-known naturalist, and Mr Strong confirmed that it was. Clearly then, Eliza was aware of Henry's fame and she went to the Brethren room to hear him preach and then walked back to Sandhurst with Henry, Edmund and Mr Curtis. Henry mentioned to Mr Curtis that Bible classes were held at Sandhurst and that he and any friends would be very welcome to attend. 'We returned to the cottage, well pleased with the minister and his courteous and kind manner to us as strangers.'

Henry was now in a very productive phase of writing and researching for *The Romance of Natural History* and *Actinologia Britannica*, and Eliza describes the many aquaria that were present in the large sitting room at Sandhurst. She also recalls Henry's energetic trips to collect materials, accompanied by Edmund, to the obvious pleasure of both. The enthusiasm carried over into his meetings with the Brightwens, and Henry had lent Eliza and her sister copies of his books, which 'formed an interesting topic of conversation during his increasingly frequent visits to the cottage.' He brought his microscope and entertained all present with various 'natural history objects', all described to the willing audience. Everyone was delighted by these visits, just as they were when they all made excursions to the local rocky shores. For the bashful Henry it provided a form of courtship and we know that his good spirits of the time had already fed back into his rekindled enthusiasm for writing. This seems to be especially so of both the content and style of *The Romance of Natural History*, which is free of unnecessary restraint. To Eliza, he was important both for his work in Natural History and for his role as the head of the local Brethren group; she also saw that he was a kind and loving father to Edmund.

Eliza describes Henry's approach in Bible classes, where parts of the text which could not be explained were met with acceptance, yet any conflicts between the literal Bible and secular views were met with vigorous opposition:

He manifested the same eager and enthusiastic spirit in his study of Divine things, as in his scientific pursuits. He studied the Bible as he would study a science. He must know what each separate portion was about, who the inspired writer was, what he was wishing to say, and for what purpose it was written; also how it was connected by prophecy or quotation with the New Testament, either in the Gospels or in the

Epistles. He was microscopic in his readings, and in his interpretations of the Word of God, for he most implicitly believed every word of the original languages to be Divine, and dictated and written, through the writers, by the Holy Ghost. These languages, through their antiquity, are necessarily obscure; thus he was content to leave many passages and even chapters unexplained, satisfied that they never contradicted each other. Where two sides of a doctrine or subject are decidedly stated, he would reverently stand, and say, "There they are! I cannot put them together, but God can. I leave it to Him and am silent. Only through the Holy Spirit can it be received into the heart."

Hence they met at these Bible classes, at meetings of the Brethren, and on Natural History visits. Eliza was impressed with him and Henry enchanted with her. Although her sister left in July, Eliza stayed on in Torquay, attending the new Brethren chapel in Fore Street, St Marychurch. Her contact with Henry and Edmund thus continued until she left Torquay on 3 September 1860 to stay with her uncle and aunt in Frome, Somerset. On 6 September she received a letter from Henry in which he proposed marriage and, 'after a week or two of consideration and consulting my friends' she accepted. They were married in Frome on 18 December and travelled immediately by train to Torquay, arriving at Sandhurst in the evening. Eliza was received warmly by Edmund, and Henry made her feel very much at home, showing his humour and sense of fun, known fully only to his intimate circle. This relaxed side of Henry's nature was never as evident as it was at this time, but the seriousness of his religious beliefs still dominated the life of the household.

Eliza did what she could to help Henry in his research and writing and she relates that he was always an early riser and worked industriously. She also realised that he was reticent in meeting others and declared 'I have no small talk' when Eliza encouraged him to go out and meet people. He did visit members of the Brethren and Eliza accompanied him until, as we have seen from Edmund's description, he found this too testing, despite being held in esteem and much admired. Visits by the three Gosses to the shore were much more enjoyable affairs and, while Henry and Edmund collected, Eliza would either watch them through field glasses, read or sketch. Like me, Henry seemed much more at home with Nature than with people that he did not know well. How many times have I used the same excuse that I have no small talk when having to take part in social events? Although somewhat cut off from the secular world, Henry took *The Times* daily and this kept him informed of contemporary events, even if many of these were treated with open scorn. Articles provided him with the opportunity to attack modern decadence and, as Henry saw it, the descent from a belief in higher truths. However, the counterpoint to this anger was that by perusing *The Times*, Henry could use the articles and maps as a method of teaching Edmund about the countries and places mentioned.

In 1864, Eliza inherited property and it meant that Henry was no longer dependent on writing and lecturing for income. This period coincided with Henry's new leisure interest in orchids and the couple also undertook some limited travel. Henry took Edmund to London in 1866 to begin his work at the British Museum and Henry and Eliza made a trip to Poole in 1868. This was a nostalgic return for Henry, who visited old family haunts and also those he had visited with his friend John Brown. The couple sketched together and painted water colours, one of which was finished at Sandhurst and hung in the dining room, reminding Henry of his boyhood roots. A trip was also made on to Dartmoor in 1869, but, mostly, Henry preferred to stay at, or close to, home. Among visitors was William Berger, the friend from the Brethren group in Hackney and a link to a key time in Henry's religious life; a further exercise in nostalgia witnessed by Eliza. The influence and character of William Berger are described movingly in Appendix II of *The Naturalist of the Sea-Shore*, written by Henry in February 1888, shortly before he died.

The various maladies and psychosomatic complaints that

plagued Henry over the past decades were now joined by more serious illnesses, with rheumatism in his hands and knees affecting him so badly that he ceased the Sandhurst Bible studies for a time and even gave up going to Brethren meetings. After treatments at Turkish baths, the rheumatism eased and Henry was able to follow his routine of collecting. It was a time that Eliza recalls with added enthusiasm and she writes:

> My husband was a true naturalist, and the fact that for many years he got his livelihood by writing books on natural history, wandering among the rocks and pools, mingling all his thoughts and sympathies with the God who formed these wonderful varieties of creation, gave a zest to his life which sedentary reading or authorship in his study could never have realized. As Kingsley has said, "Happy truly is the naturalist! He has no time for melancholy dreams. The earth becomes transparent; everywhere he sees significance, harmonies, laws, chains of cause and effect endlessly interlinked, which draw him out of the narrow sphere of self into a pure and wholesome region of joy and wonder."

That resonates still, even to those who don't believe in a God as fully as Henry, or to those who don't believe in a God at all.

Eliza ends her narrative by describing her impressions of Henry's final years, after he had 'mischief of the heart' (congestive cardiopulmonary disease) and became increasingly incapacitated. He began to lose interest in his work and in other things although, as we know from Edmund, he was able to make occasional short trips out. The final paragraph contains the sentence: 'As to the influence of his life and teaching on … future generations, "the day" [Judgement Day] alone will declare it.' We await that event, but nevertheless can consider the life of Henry Gosse, and his achievements, in a contemporary context. Before turning to that topic, it is pertinent to mention a contemporary of Henry Gosse, William Pengelly, who also held deeply-held Christian beliefs. In spite of these experiences in common, William's views were not like Henry's, yet both believed in the same God and the same Bible.

William Pengelly; a friend of Henry Gosse and a deeply religious man who believed in 'creation by evolution'

William Pengelly and Henry Gosse both lived in Torquay for most of their adult lives and there were several similarities in their backgrounds. William was born in Looe, Cornwall on 12 January 1812, and was thus nearly the same age as Henry and both shared a love of the sea. William worked full-time on his father's boat, so his interest was as a seaman as well as a Natural Historian.

Sarah Pengelly (née Prout), William's mother, was an artist, as was Henry's father, and she was 'from the same family' as Samuel Prout the famous watercolourist, much admired by John Ruskin and by members of the Royal Family. Although William had little formal education, this did not prevent him learning from books and, like Henry, he had a spell as a schoolmaster and founder of his own school. His fame came from his contributions to Geology however, and he was one of the co-founders of the Torquay Natural History Society, renowned as a centre for those interested in cave exploration. William became a deeply religious Quaker and a strong teetotaller but, unlike Henry, was 'an early convert to the theory of creation by evolution' to quote from Hester Pengelly's *A Memoir of William Pengelly*. [7] In the same section of the memoir, Henry Gosse is described as 'a staunch exponent of the literal Mosaic doctrine of creation.' This contrast in their stance on Creation reflected the differences in attitude, and approach to life, between Quakers and members of the Brethren; the former being more accepting of changes in interpretation of events than the latter.

Both William and Henry knew personal tragedy, as William's

first wife died young and his eldest son did not survive infancy. His wife had always been in poor health and this caused William to suffer 'much anxiety', but Hester describes him as having a 'keen sense of humour, high spirits and love of fun.' His open nature enabled William to make close friendships with other scientists and E. Ray Lankester, who knew both William and Henry, described a further acquaintance as being 'most pleasant, and a very interesting and enthusiastic man, something like Pengelly in manner.' [8] William enjoyed increasing recognition for his excavations of human remains found in caves in Torquay and Brixham where, by careful examination and removal of strata, he had shown the coexistence of humans with prehistoric animals, when Britain was linked physically to the European continent. Some of these animals, like the mammoth, were now extinct, pointing to the antiquity of humans.

Among the closest of William's friendships was with Sir Charles Lyell, who championed the concept of changes occurring though geological time and was a considerable influence on Darwin and the development of the ideas leading to *The Origin of Species*. In contrast, Henry Gosse did not like Lyell, although he did get on well with Darwin. It wasn't because of the backgrounds of the two men, as both Lyell and Darwin were from wealthy families and both were educated at University. Perhaps Henry felt empathy with Darwin because he sensed he was a fellow sufferer from psychosomatic illness and that both had known personal tragedy?

As William and Henry lived in Torquay, it was inevitable that they would meet on occasions, and one can assume that their conversation skirted around certain subjects. However, they each had great energy in collecting, observing and writing and were meticulous and accurate observers. These were typical Victorian traits, but both Henry and William seemed especially industrious. In a letter from the second Mrs Pengelly (née Lydia Spriggs) to her mother dated 11 November 1857 (about the time of the publication of *Omphalos*, and quoted in Hester's biography) she writes: 'William went [on] a very pleasant excursion down the Dart yesterday, with Mr Gosse, the Naturalist. We see a good deal of him, he is an exquisite artist in his own line ...'. This comment not only shows the respect for Henry's ability but also the regularity of contact between the two men at this time.

A further record of their friendship comes in a letter of March 1859 following a visit to a cavern south of Berry Head near Brixham, in the company of several other enthusiasts. No fossils were found on this expedition and William returned with Henry and the others and there followed 'many interesting anecdotes about natural history, one story seeming to call out half a dozen others.' One can imagine how the shared enthusiasm of the group led to such an evening and, in the same letter, Lydia Pengelly also refers to Edmund as 'a nice boy' and it is clear that he was very much involved in the friendship between Henry and William. We read that 'Gosse called here and had a chat this afternoon' on 26 June 1859, suggesting that the two men enjoyed a relaxed and informal friendship and this was the time of Henry's recovery from grief and the negative reactions to *Omphalos*. The *Romance of Natural History* was in preparation and Henry had just published *Evenings at the Microscope*. He was soon to meet Eliza Brightwen and, for him, was at his most outgoing.

The final reference to Henry in Hester's memoir of her father comes in a quote from a letter sent by one of William's ex-pupils in 1863, the year when he was elected an FRS and when the student responded to a suggestion that his old teacher may leave Torquay:

My first feeling on reading the latter part of your letter was one of such *intense selfishness*, that I would not let myself write for a few days, till I could say that *if you leave Torquay for your own advantage*, I shall be glad of it, though I shall miss you more than any friend you have there ... Tell me what to look for near Lewes in the Chalk. I mean to work very hard; can I get anything for you? I don't care for Mr Gosse or his book; or anything, till I hear whether we are to lose you.

The book referred to in the letter must have been *Omphalos*.

1 Thwaite, A, *Glimpses of the Wonderful: The Life of Philip Henry Gosse*, (Faber and Faber), London, 2002.

2 Gosse, E, *Father and Son. A Study of Two Temperaments*, (William Heinemann), London, 1907. Reprinted, (Penguin), London, 1986.

3 *Bradshaw's Descriptive Railway Hand-Book of Great Britain and Ireland*. Produced in facsimile edition by Old House Books, Oxford 2012.

4 Gosse, E, *The Naturalist of the Sea-Shore; The Life of Philip Henry Gosse*, (William Heinemann), London, 1890.

5 Thwaite, A. *Edmund Gosse: A Literary Landscape*, (Tempus Publishing), Stroud, 2007.

6 Gosse, E, *Shakespeare to Pope: an enquiry into the causes and phenomena of the rise of classical poetry in England*, (Dodd, Mead and Company), London, 1885.

7 Pengelly, H, (ed.), *A Memoir of William Pengelly, of Torquay, F.R.S., Geologist, with a selection from his correspondence*, (John Murray), London, 1897.

8 Lester, J, and Bowler, P. J., *E. Ray Lankester and the Making of Modern British Biology*, British Society for the History of Science Monograph, (Alden Press), Oxford, 1995.

Back to the Present

Henry Gosse and the negativity of religious faith

For I have learned
To look on nature, not as in the hour
Of thoughtless youth; but hearing oftentimes
The still, sad music of humanity,
Nor harsh nor grating, though of ample power
To chasten and subdue. And I have felt
A presence that disturbs me with the joy
Of elevated thoughts; a sense sublime
Of something far more deeply interfused,
Whose dwelling is the light of setting suns,
And the round ocean and the living air,
And the blue sky, and in the mind of man:
A motion and a spirit, that impels
All thinking things, all objects of all thought,
And rolls through all things. Therefore am I still
A lover of the meadows and the woods,
And mountains; and of all that we behold
From this green earth; of all the mighty world
Of eye, and ear – both what they half create,
And what perceive; well pleased to recognise
In nature and the language of the sense
The anchor of my purest thoughts, the nurse,
The guide, the guardian of my heart, and soul
Of all my moral being.

Extract from *Lines Composed a Few Miles above Tintern Abbey, On Revisiting the Banks of the Wye during a Tour*, William Wordsworth, 1798.

*M*uch of what we know about Henry Gosse's life comes from the two biographies written by Edmund and, especially the second, *Father and Son*, which details the difficult relationship between the two men. It is not uncommon for a father and son to go through phases of intolerance and misunderstanding, as I know from my own upbringing and at the expense of some pain and guilt.

In writing about Henry's personal life, there is thus a bias to overcome, especially as Edmund's views on his father are so well known. *Father and Son* is regarded so highly that it has been a set book in English Literature courses and was the basis of the play *Where Adam Stood* by the playwright and dramatist, Dennis Potter. [1] Neither the book, nor the play, cast Henry in a good light and it is easy to have sympathy for the way Edmund felt. Even so, I also feel sympathy for Henry, a good man with outstanding talents, yet the victim of his own rigid views.

Nobody can question Henry Gosse's love of Nature and his ability to communicate what he saw in words and pictures. As a result of these talents, I can share his sense of wonder in observing the natural world and, in researching and writing this book, I have grown close to Henry and what he achieved, but I suspect that we would be exasperated with one another's religious beliefs should we have met. It is tempting to suggest that I would be the more accommodating, but that may not be so. Henry painted himself into a corner, with his need to be unquestioning about the literal truth of everything handed down to us in The Bible. While Henry's faith was all important to him, and sustained him, it was to be a destructive force on his reputation and on the life of some of those around him. It went over the boundaries of 'this is right for me' to 'this is right' to 'this is right, everyone who doesn't share this view is wrong.' It isn't only Christians, or other theists, that cross these boundaries of acceptability of course, and I always find this attitude unsettling.

There are many aspects of the lives of Henry and Edmund Gosse, and the conflict in their positions, which are relevant today, and which contribute to contemporary debates. In exploring these, I rather boldly make unwritten pleas against religious extremism, for tolerance of opposing views, and for appreciating Natural History, something which we can all share. My approach is, of course, shaped by my own background and experiences.

Henry Gosse was a typical Victorian man, being Head of the Household and having a wife who was subservient to him; this was true of both Emily and Eliza, although Emily was a moderating counsellor and Henry clearly took her opinion into consideration. Both women recognised that Henry was a great and talented man and Emily enjoyed the celebration of his achievements by Learned Societies, ended abruptly by her final illness and death. Eliza encouraged Henry to meet with more of society but, by then, he was becoming the 'troglodyte', and more and more firmly entrenched in his rather isolated existence.

Henry's life was dominated by his immovable Christian faith, by his membership of the Brethren and, more specifically, by his being the leader of his own admiring congregation. My only contact with the Brethren was with the two leaders of the Crusaders group which I attended after leaving Winner Street Baptist Church and, while they were both kind men, they certainly wanted us to share their beliefs. From Henry's writings, it is clear that both the Brethren and Baptists follow the practice of adult baptism by immersion and have a deep dislike of Catholicism. In spite of these shared beliefs, they took different paths and why religions break up into sects has always been a puzzle to me. Of course, schism is easy to understand when it is associated with power, and the Protestant antagonism towards Catholicism has been a feature of European History for centuries. But why are there so many sects, with their associated deep distrust and even dislike, when belief is in the same God and everything that is known is based on the same Holy Scriptures? The argument is the same for branches of Islam, having the Koran as a guide, or for the differing approaches of Judaism, with the Torah common to all. If seen in biological terms, the intolerance that generates sects is the driving force for keeping the groups separate, like physical or behavioural barriers between sub-populations that eventually lead to new species. But why does it happen in religion?

As an adult, Henry was intolerant of any questioning of his beliefs. His earlier views on the 'evil' of Catholicism were, much like my own, inherited, but then reinforced by the noisy and rebellious Catholic residents of Newfoundland. They made him feel vulnerable, and this feeling was enhanced both by being far from home and by the anxiety he felt over the serious illness of his sister Elizabeth, her recovery being clear evidence to him of the power of prayer. Henry's vulnerability thus made him susceptible to conversion to the religious views of Mr and Mrs Jaques, with God as the centre of their existence. Yet, it was only after his full time return to England, the experience of rejection in love, and the presence of hard times, that Henry became fully radical in his beliefs. His subsequent discovery of the imminence of The Second Coming, and the need to be prepared at all times for this event, now dominated his life. By confining himself to meetings of like believers, his views were reinforced and there was no turning back. Henry's religious beliefs (and the anxiety that came with them) were pivotal in his reaction to the three key challenges in his life: the illness and death of Emily; the upbringing of Edmund and the threat (as he saw it) to Biblical Creation provided by mid-nineteenth century thought. It is for the second that he is best known, although members of the scientific community might disagree and, in truth, Henry Gosse is largely a forgotten figure. He doesn't deserve this fate.

Our knowledge of Henry's beliefs comes from his books and, especially, the factual account in the first biography and the less accurate second biography (largely autobiography) by

Edmund. As Henry was to meet with Emily after death, it was his strongest wish that Edmund would be with them and with Eliza. It became increasingly clear that, whatever Edmund's own religious beliefs, they were not those of a member of the Brethren and thus there could be no guarantee that he would be saved, despite having cleared the first hurdle when he underwent adult baptism as a child. Henry must have been worried constantly about this; more than is normal in a relationship between father and son. It's where I derive the feeling that he was imprisoned by his religious beliefs, as well as being supported by them. It all seems too awful and, although I broke away from organised religion and never went back, I can certainly empathise with what Henry and Edmund went through. There was no pressure on me to conform to the Christian views of our family, but for Edmund it was continuous and intense. It is pleasing to know that there was a degree of reconciliation between father and son at the end of Henry's life, at a time when he was too ill and tired to allow his religious self to keep up the effort of working on his son. In contrast to Edmund, Nellie Gosse felt warmly towards Henry and her feelings were reciprocated. It was easier for her not to be in open conflict, as she wasn't part of the upbringing which marked both Edmund and Henry, although we must not forget the very happy times the two spent together on the shores near St Marychurch, and in looking though materials they collected. Edmund and Nellie's children must also have been a joy to them all.

Did Henry die happily? We don't know the answer, but a belief in the imminent Second Coming seems like a way of avoiding the prospect of dying. He may have been scared of death, as we all are to a greater or lesser extent and this would also explain, in part, his passion for looking at living things. It wasn't just the wonder of Creation and evidence of the magnificence of God, but also a way of appreciating just what life is and that it comes to an end. Maybe, deep down, that was my motive for going on country walks at the time my mother's and father's funerals and subsequent cremations. It was a selfish act, but also a form of avoiding acceptance of what had happened; I was both running away from their deaths and towards something that seemed permanent, yet changing. Could this be why Natural History has had such a hold over me, and something which continues to this day?

Creation, Evolution and the Origin of Life

Henry's conflict with mid-nineteenth century thought further encouraged the sense of isolation that came from his religious views. As the scientific community accepted the existence of geological time scales, Henry felt forced to defend his belief in the literal Biblical account of Creation. *Omphalos* was the result and his personal revelation of prochronic existence alienated those on both sides of the debate. From believing he had 'untied the geological knot', he found that the response of his audience ranged from hostility to something verging on mockery.

In considering how *Omphalos* was received by the scientific community, we need to understand something of the mores of the times. Although Henry had not been to University, his meticulous research was recognised by the award of Fellowship of the Royal Society and he was respected by his fellow members of the Learned Societies of the time. This was certainly merited and his scientific works continued to be used more than a hundred years after their publication.

Henry would have been aware of the debate that occurred over the views of Lamarck, published in 1809. Lamarck had suggested that characteristics acquired during the life of an organism could be passed to the next generation and this was, of course, a form of evolution. Evolution was not a new idea, as Erasmus Darwin had proposed it at the end of the eighteenth century, but Lamarck believed that spontaneous generation occurred continuously, with new species then embarking on the process of change through transformation. His theory gained little credence, but Robert Grant at the University of London was a notable supporter. For this, Grant was frozen out by the Scientific Establishment. Among the attackers was T. H. Huxley, who seems to have been a man with little respect for opposing views and was prepared to fight hard for those whose ideas he supported, most notably Charles Darwin, who had been one of Grant's students when they were both at the University of Edinburgh. These attacks were indicative of the strength of feeling in scientific circles in the 1830s to 1850s. It is easy to see how those with powerful egos strove to achieve dominance and thus power for their faction, just as they continue to do today. This was the background for the launch of *Omphalos*, which was probably regarded as a sincere attempt, but one which was clearly too idiosyncratic to be taken seriously. Much the same view as we have today, although distance in time from publication allows us to admire the folly of it all. Of course, Henry Gosse was not a threat to anyone, so it wouldn't have become really vicious, and Darwin's major contribution to the evolution debate was published just two years after *Omphalos*. *The Origin of Species* changed our thinking forever, and not just in scientific circles. Evolution by natural selection is a cornerstone of contemporary Biology and cannot be easily removed.

If the Biblical view of Creation is unlikely, thereby dooming *Omphalos* as unnecessary, how did the events described metaphorically in Genesis come about? Life originated on Earth billions of years ago and the first living organisms were single-celled and probably resembled the most primitive bacteria known today. So how do we define life? That's a philosophical point that has been debated many times but, to me, it must reflect the formation of an entity that is able to receive nutrients from its environment and which is able to reproduce. Others might suggest that the origin of life comes with the aggregation of molecules which are able to replicate and produce chemicals like proteins that we know are a feature of organisms, which we all agree are living. Whatever one's definition, it would seem that there was a point when the critical step to a living form occurred and the key question then is whether this was a singular event, or whether it occurred many times.

Let's consider that the origin of life, whatever it was, happened on many occasions. If so, were all these appearances of life simultaneous or separated by time, perhaps even occurring today? Of course, we don't know the answer but, if there were many occasions when life appeared, it is not difficult to extend the idea to the possibility that life also exists elsewhere in the Universe, if conditions are appropriate. The likelihood of such events occurring elsewhere increases the more times the event occurred on Earth. Many astrobiologists are happy to sign up to this idea and feel that it is a matter of time before we discover life elsewhere, whatever life means. There is no evidence to support such a view.

As we don't know how life began, can we know where the event was likely to have occurred? The answer is obviously no, but that has not stopped the suggestion that life originated at an alkaline hydrothermal vent, these structures being features of regions of the deep oceans that were unknown until the latter part of the twentieth century. That life originated around alkaline hydrothermal vents is now accepted as fact in some quarters, so often is the suggestion repeated. I'm sceptical and, although conditions around these vents provide an environment that is ideal for the production of some essential precursors of life, their assembly may easily have occurred elsewhere. But where? We know that conditions on Earth were very different indeed four billion years ago compared to today, so it all comes down to guesswork. I would plump for the water-atmosphere surface film, or the surface of a gas bubble, somewhere near a land mass having high volcanic activity.

If life began in a single event, an event so extraordinarily rare that it was never repeated, we must conclude that it is unlikely to have occurred elsewhere. Molecular evolution attempts to trace all life forms back to a single ancestor but, of course, we do not know if this single ancestor was just that, or whether there were lots of single ancestors all appearing in the same geological time period. The idea of a once only event does not imply that the origin of life was driven by a theistic force (although that cannot be ruled out), but a moment of such immense significance has the power of the supernatural.

Of course, all considerations of this kind were irrelevant to creationists like Henry Gosse. There are still many people who cannot believe in the evolution of all the living forms which we have in the world today, and those we know from fossil forms, beginning with the moment when chemicals formed into a cell. Creationists usually believe in the near simultaneous appearance of all life forms, and Henry was certainly of this view (although he was also fully aware of geological time scales – the conflict being resolved by the idea of prochronic existence). The debate between creationists and evolutionists continues, sometimes in heated discussion, and, although I am an atheist and evolutionist, how can I teach Biology in a way that does not offend creationists? Should I even bother to try? Some suggest that all talk of creation should be squashed, based as it is on the supernatural, but I want to be inclusive. We can all marvel at Natural History, whatever our explanations for the existence of living things, and this is a view that has been reinforced by studying Henry Gosse, one of the great Natural Historians. Paradoxically, Henry was not capable of such apparent tolerance.

When believing in Creation can seem like an easy option

Some adaptations of contemporary organisms are so extraordinary that it is easier to believe that they were created rather than evolved by a series of chance events. Let me give two examples from an exceptionally long list.

Female bolas spiders spin a silk thread which terminates in a sticky blob of silk and this is used to capture passing moths. Well, not just passing, as the female spiders also secrete a chemical which mimics those produced by female moths, thus attracting in the males and making capture easier. So, we have an organism with an external, jointed skeleton which has sense organs, the ability to anaesthetise prey, that has mouthparts to chop up the captured moths, that has a complex system of chemicals which are used to digest parts of the prey, that takes up the products of digestion and, add to that, a sophisticated system that attracts the prey before capture using a device 'designed' for the job. This is only part of the extraordinary make-up of female bolas spiders. But how did all that evolve? I love asking that question, as it teaches one that such complexity must have required many small steps or, perhaps, some large ones. Each successful change, the result of a genetic mutation, would then allow increased chances of survival for individuals and thus be passed to future generations. But how did the ability to produce analogues of the hormones produced by female moths arise? Certainly, creation almost seems the easier explanation here, with it all resulting from organisation by a very busy God. That's certainly how Henry Gosse would have understood it.

A bolas spider with silk 'blob'. (Image courtesy of Matt Coors).

Like spiders, some insects produce silk, perhaps as a means of cementing cases for protection, or as a means of producing a cocoon, like silk moths, in which they can form into a pupa and then transform into adults. A less well-known example of insect silk is that produced by larval blackflies; not the aphids of gardens, but the immature stages of a biting fly, common in high latitudes and also in tropical countries. Blackfly larvae live in streams and rivers and produce two types of silk: pads which are used for attachment and which allow them to move over substrata like inchworms; and threads which act as lifelines if they are swept away in fast water. Larvae look a bit like worms with a head capsule and close observation of the head shows that it bears two filtering fans that capture particles from the water passing over the larvae. Particles as small as one ten thousandth of a millimetre are captured, and everything which has been collected is swept to the mouth when the feeding fans are folded. These fans are beautifully engineered, extending by hydraulic pressure and folding by the use of a single muscle. After some weeks of larval growth, during which there are moults resulting in new sets of fans each time, the insects produce a cocoon of silk (yet another use of this valuable material) and change into a pupa from which the adult emerges to fly free from the water, each fly emerging in a gas bubble. It is not wetted and can fly away immediately after breaking the water surface. Male and female adult blackflies feed on plant sugars to gain energy for flight, but the females usually have to bite animals to obtain a blood meal, as they cannot develop eggs without the ingredients in blood. The mouthparts of adult flies are thus very different indeed to the feeding organs of larvae. How did this extraordinary suite of characteristics evolve, complete with a total lifestyle change between larvae, pupa and adults?

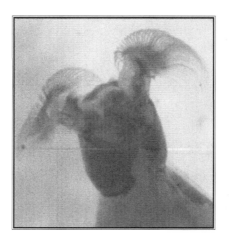

Head of a larval blackfly showing the head fans.
(From Author's Collection).

While creation provides an easy answer to the diversity of life forms and behaviours which we see around us, we have to think about who is attempting the explanation of how the diversity arose. Humans love myths and we also comprehend a very limited time scale. We think in years and decades when dealing with our immediate family, and centuries at most when thinking of our national history, anything at the millennial scale being difficult to comprehend in any real sense. When we are young, a year is a long time – how many times have you heard a small child say that they are, say, 6½ years old or even 6¾? As an old person, I look back over several decades and, while memories are clear, any film footage of events from the 1950s and 60s makes me realise just how times have changed; what immediate history feels like. Going back generations seems almost a trip to the unknown and most people in the western world calculate years from the time Christ was supposed to have been born and this, too, seems very long ago; almost into what we call ancient history. Yet it is very recent indeed in geological time and we are likely to witness only small changes in most organisms in our life time, or even in the period of human history. Of course, there are exceptions to this general point, as demonstrated by the development of resistance to antibiotics shown by bacteria; the result of short generation times and very large numbers of organisms able to undergo mutations.

If we could sense geological time, the wonder of evolution – 'The Magic of Reality', to quote Richard Dawkins – might be diminished. It is this wonder that propelled Darwin's thinking and it has a power like that of a religious belief. We know that life began, and that it has undergone myriad changes, but we wonder because we cannot understand time. Maybe that is why a theistic interpretation feels more comfortable for some? To me, evolution provides the best explanation, although I have no idea how evolutionary changes that produced the extraordinary diversity around us came about. All from an original single cell, too.

Tackling the supernatural

Myths grow as our best attempts to explain the apparently inexplicable. Henry Gosse attempted explanations of mythical creatures such as unicorns, sea serpents and mermaids, believing that the myths surrounding them had a natural origin. I share the same interest, extending it to stories in The Bible, and one example is my article 'The Ten Plagues of Egypt' published in *Opticon1826*.[2] My source was Exodus, chapters 7 to 11 in the King James' Bible. Deliberately, I decided not to read commentaries on the Plagues that have been written by other authors, as I didn't want these to influence my own interpretation of the descriptions given.

It was possible to explain the first nine Plagues by natural events, but an explanation for the tenth – the death of the firstborn – eluded me, and remains a mystery. I suggested that the Plagues were manifestations of a sequence of very unusual climatic conditions; with heavy rains, droughts and strong winds all occurring in a short time scale and having a big effect on populations of plants and animals. The strength of each event was so rare that it caused consternation among the population in much of the Nile Valley at that time. Of course, it is not entirely impossible that the sequence of disasters was organised by a theistic force and, if so, the Plagues were intended to be awe-inspiring, especially as they followed each other in rapid succession. It is not my view, but it is a possible explanation and I said so in the article.

The ideas expressed in the article were taken up by *The Times* under the headline: 'Plagues of Egypt "caused by nature, not God"'. I had not written that and felt a little indignant, but that shows my naiveté about what makes a good story in the press. There followed a series of blogs and reports from people on both atheistic and religious websites and I confess that my ego was boosted initially by this recognition. However, very few of those who wrote seemed to have read the original article and even fewer had considered what it contained. Most reacted just to the headline in *The Times*, even though the piece as a whole was well-written and was certainly based on a thorough reading of my article. I wonder what Henry Gosse's reaction would have been? He wouldn't have complained about my use of the King James' Bible as a source, and he was content to recognise that some of the Bible's contents were inexplicable to us and that we had to take them at face value. That's what I did, of course, but I surmise Henry would not have agreed with my interpretation, coming as it did from someone who wasn't of his exclusive religious persuasion.

Another article on a mythological topic, entitled 'Angels, putti, dragons and fairies: Believing the impossible', was also published in *Opticon1826*, [3] and in it I considered how such winged creatures (humans, except for dragons?) might fly. Angels have bird wings according to popular imagery, yet there is no record in the King James' Bible of angels having wings at all, that is if cherubim and seraphim are excluded from this category. Putti also have bird wings, but very tiny ones; fairies have insect wings, and dragons have wings that are most closely modelled on those of bats. At least that is what the illustrative arts will have us believe.

After examining the flight mechanism of birds, insects and bats it is clear that angels, putti, fairies and dragons cannot fly in the same way as their animal counterparts and must use some supernatural power. Now, if one doesn't believe in supernatural power then it isn't possible to believe in these winged forms and certainly not in the use of their wings for powered flight. This simple conclusion once again seemed to stir up much popular comment in the media and on the internet, but the interest was focussed entirely on angels; barely anyone mentioned the other creatures. Clearly, people want to believe in angels with bird wings and even some of those with sincere religious faith are in that camp. True, it is impossible to visit any church or cemetery without seeing bird-winged angels aplenty, but they owe their appearance not to any Holy Word but to the images of Greek deities on which the statues, carvings and paintings were modelled originally. Flighted forms are portrayed to allow us to believe in links to other Worlds; whether Heaven, a pleasant underworld or a place of evil. Some of us have a need to feel connected to such places. What would Henry have thought of angels, for he must have believed in them, whatever their form?

What happened to Dr Dryasdust?

Returning to the rather more mundane world of academic science, I come to Dr Dryasdust. He was used by Henry Gosse in the Preface of *The Romance of Natural History [First Series]* as a metaphor for classical Zoologists of the time, usually based in museums throughout the World, who made detailed observations on dead organisms. Their work, and that of their counterparts in universities, formed the basis of the academic discipline of Zoology, being the knowledge of animal types and their detailed structure and function. There are still scientists working in this way today, but they are uncommon, and Zoology has undergone a transformation in the last fifty years. Before this, there were few changes in approach to those of Henry Gosse's time, although we did have the addition of biochemistry, genetics, and, of course, evolution.

Coming to the twenty-first century, Zoology and Botany are still studied as distinct disciplines, but Biology is now taught more commonly as a single subject. The revolution has come from the introduction of molecular and genetic approaches that attempt to provide a mechanistic view of living things. It is a shift in focus from the organism to the molecules inside individual cells, and this part of the contemporary subject has been termed Modern Biology by some. Modern Biology attempts to reduce organisms to a series of chemical reactions, controlled by genes within each cell, the environment then only rarely extending beyond the cell membrane. It is a long way from Natural History and from classical Botany and Zoology.

Biology has also drawn closer to Medicine, and our interest has been more and more on humans. This excessive focus on our own species has turned us into navel-gazers or, to use a bad pun, 'omphalos-gazers', and I hope that Modern Biology achieves the results expected of it. Certainly, there will be many further successes in gaining understanding of how our bodies work, although progress is accompanied by the risk of finding little other than a large quantity of data. This could be viewed as a facetious comment, yet there is a huge amount of biomedical research being conducted globally. These endeavours certainly provide a catalyst for the development of new treatments in medicine and in the discovery of novel drugs, and this is important in health care. But there is a great deal of money to be made from this work, which surely explains why there is so much media coverage of cures for various diseases being on the horizon. It may be done to keep funding streams open, especially as the focus is on two of the realities of human life that worry us most – ageing and dying – but there will be increasing questioning of whether the money is well spent and whether sufficient money is being generated. Hopefully, the quantity of medical and biomedical research will diminish as we recognise that quality rather than quantity is more significant, and that there are more ways to maintain health than in understanding genes. After all, epidemiologists tell us repeatedly that the environment in which people live has an important impact on their health, as does their sense of emotional well-being. Having an interest in Natural History and the nature of the world around us must have a part to play in the equation.

Both Henry and Emily Gosse would have welcomed the palliative care that is available today, using drugs that have been developed by the research of Modern Biologists. But I wonder how Henry would view their approach to the study of Biology? I have a feeling that he would find the mechanistic approach a challenge to his view of God, seeking as it does to provide an explanation for the functioning and variety of living things. Nevertheless, the latter aspect would have been welcomed by Dr Dryasdust. Looking at the genetic structure of organisms allows us to see their relatedness, in the same way that we can look at the relatedness and ancestry of human populations. This has opened new approaches to the classification of micro-organisms, plants and animals, which had previously been based solely on morphological and anatomical features. We can analyse how closely related an organism of one species is to an organism of a different species and trace each back to their parental stock. Of course, we did this in classical Zoology and Botany, but the advent of analyses based on the chemicals of inheritance has transformed everything. It has taken away the opinion of experts with their accumulated knowledge and replaced it with statistical probability. Even so, it does require experts to interpret the lineages and family trees that result.

Probably the most important development for the successors of Dr Dryasdust has been routine usage of PCR (polymerase chain reaction) that allows us to manufacture quantities of DNA, the basis of each genetic blueprint, for analysis from tiny amounts of the original. This means that even the DNA of fossils can be used, although care must be taken to avoid the effects of contamination. We have moved from the microscope, callipers and dissection of the earlier era to the contemporary use of complex machines, but microscopes and the means of measurement are still needed. They, too, have become much more sophisticated with the advances made in electronics and computation, and we can now store images, enhance them, and compare them in detail using computer programs. It takes us away from the artistry of illustrators like Henry Gosse and, arguably, from the powers of observation that such artists need. I wonder if this is a good thing?

If approaches to studying Botany and Zoology have been transformed, what of the museums with which many Victorian biologists were associated; the colleagues whom Henry so strongly encouraged to go outside and view organisms in their natural environment? At UCL, the Grant Museum of Zoology shows how much has changed since Henry's time, yet how much has remained the same. It was founded by Robert Grant and he was the first Professor of Comparative Anatomy at the time the College was founded in 1827 as the University of London, holding the Chair until his death in 1874. Grant was succeeded by E. Ray Lankester in 1875 and it was he who asked Edmund Gosse to write the first biography of Henry. Grant was a medical doctor, but made his name from the study of sponges and, like Henry Gosse, made observations at the shore. On starting his teaching career at the University of London, Grant had no material to illustrate his many lectures, so started to collect preserved specimens, skeletons and papers. This teaching collection, with additions made by Lankester and others, provides the basis for the current Grant Museum which continues its important role in research and teaching today. It is now open to the public and is one of the gems of London's museum world, where visitors see the skeletons and bottled specimens alongside modern display material and VDUs, a change that has occurred in all Natural History museums. So much more is now done to disseminate information for visitors, although this might erode their child-like ability to ask questions about what they see. It's that child-like questioning that forms the basis of learning.

My interest in teaching and lecturing

Whatever the pronouncements made on the subject by senior academics, teaching in universities today has a lower status than research activity, although they should be regarded as being equally important. Despite its diminished status (or do I mean because of it?), I enjoy teaching and consider it a privilege to work with students. It's another area where I empathise with Henry, although I cannot claim to be in his league when it comes to the use of illustrations.

The first step in my teaching career came when I was appointed to a full-time Demonstratorship in Zoology at the University of Newcastle-upon-Tyne. It was a three-year post that allowed me to develop the research I had done for my Doctorate at Durham

University and I also had to teach dissection classes and give lectures. I think I landed the job because I had been complimented on my work as a teaching assistant in practical classes, and on field courses, while I was a postgraduate at Durham, and the compliments had found their way into references. Apparently, I had the ability to explain points well and with enthusiasm. It was something that came naturally to me and may have been a skill I inherited from my father. He was always recognised as a skilled salesperson throughout his long stint at Perrett's of Paignton.

In addition to the dissection classes at Newcastle, I used the medical museum to teach parasitology, backing up these sessions with fresh material which I collected from the local abattoir. I appreciated fully the value of museums, just as I had done as an undergraduate, with the splendid Cole Museum of Zoology at Reading University. Yet, the most enjoyable contact with students was on field courses; the very kind of Natural History which Henry Gosse enjoyed teaching at Ilfracombe and Tenby. We took classes to Malham in Yorkshire and worked both on the local rivers and on the lake, Malham Tarn. I learned a lot from my colleague Athol McLachlan on those field courses; about how to teach, how to make quantitative exercises interesting, and how to encourage some reluctant students to keep working to identify the animals that we collected. Plants only received cursory treatment; something which seems odd to me now, but ours was a Department of Zoology, and Botany was still taught as a separate discipline then. Field courses of all kinds are a wonderful way to teach, as Henry knew. All the participants are involved, with the teachers guiding and lending experience, and a formal timetable cannot be used. It's no wonder they are among the most popular parts of university courses among students. There is the social contact too, of course, with everyone getting to know one another and with less of a barrier between teachers and students.

Although I had given research talks, lecturing was a new experience, and a rather frightening one. Being shy was no help and

I found standing in front of a class to be intimidating. I remember listening to my own voice (a cliché, but an accurate one) and thinking that an hour was a very long stretch of time, especially after five minutes had elapsed. I tried to use the blackboard or whiteboard, but my drawings were quite inadequate, not like those which would have been given by Henry Gosse. Overhead projection was a help, as illustrations could then be used from books, but preparing material was not easy as one had to estimate how illustrations and labels would look when projected. It all seems so distant now that we are in the age of PowerPoint and printed handouts.

The feeling of anxiety before each lecture did not subside for some time and I still felt it when I was appointed as a Lecturer at Goldsmiths' College London, following my three years at Newcastle. The build up would begin with me perspiring through nervousness and I had to slip out for a smoke. It did ease with time and, although I still feel a little nervous, I now rather enjoy lecturing. Even in the early days, I was able to get points across and offer clear explanations, and I also found that an ability to improvise came in handy. If something came into my head that seemed funny, or an anecdote seemed appropriate, out it would come, so ad-libbing was very much part of the performance. Anonymous reports on my lectures and practical classes have mostly been very good and I ended up winning awards for my teaching, something which would have surprised me when I started out.

Unlike today's new lecturers, I wasn't given any instruction in how to do the job and had to use what came naturally, and then learn from more experienced lecturers. Fortunately, in my time as a student at Reading University, we had one or two lecturers who were very good role models. Quite the best was Professor Graham who managed to weave lectures into a fascinating narrative, all delivered in his gentle Scots accent. We were in awe of him anyway, but he was inspirational, so much so that there were times when I could overcome my feeling of needing to go for a pee. Being a good lecturer is akin to being a good actor, which probably also explains the stage fright. The difference is that we write our own script and that is where I was fortunate. My lectures are largely focussed on Natural History, so it was easy to be ebullient and convey something of the child-like and open-minded sense of wonder that the subject brings. There were not many things that I share in equal measure with Henry Gosse, but enthusiasm for living organisms is certainly one. We both had that from when we were young.

Natural History and the Media

Henry Gosse was described by Stephen Jay Gould as the David Attenborough of his day, based on his books, lectures and enthusiasm for aquaria, all of which made Natural History a popular activity for many Victorians in the growing middle class. While the academic and research world has shifted to Modern Biology, Natural History remains popular with amateurs, and television programmes involving the subject attract large audiences. The advent of new camera and production techniques has brought images of all manner of plants and animals into our living rooms, or to our mobile devices. There remains a focus on larger organisms, as we have been trained to think of these as being more interesting and they are certainly the most popular subjects. Ask anyone what they remember about the *Life on Earth* television series and I'm sure that most will recall David Attenborough sitting amongst gorillas. Swimming alongside comb jellies doesn't have the same effect on our imagination.

Wonderful camera-work, and the patience of camera operators and production crews, means that exciting footage is commonplace, and it affects our view of places we visit, especially if they were locations used for recording. Our expectations are built up and we are disappointed if we see little, having expected much after our armchair view. Another adverse effect of presenting Natural History through the visual media is that television, film, and print don't provide smells, heat and cold, or humidity, so essential parts of the potential sensory experience are missing. A further feature of Natural History programmes is the need for a presenter to be on camera and the use of background music to conjure up a mood. We must have music now, especially for sequences that are already dramatic, as it heightens our emotional involvement with the scenes presented. I confess I find it very annoying but that's just me being old-fashioned and out of touch. Presenters can be even more annoying. Before the boom in visual media, we looked at Natural History films and television and an off-screen commentator explained what we saw and linked scenes. Now we have presenters as on-screen stars, almost as important as the material they front, and it is a role which can be high on the list of dream jobs for young people.

Although I appreciate Gould's comparison of Henry Gosse and David Attenborough, they are from very different ages and, from all descriptions, Henry's presenting skills were not those of the warm, polished and engaging Attenborough. I can only guess at how Henry would have dealt with being in front of a television, film or video camera. For all I know he might have been a star presenter, but somehow I doubt it, even with his wonderful ability with words.

Our need to be anthropomorphic – and why are we so interested in dinosaurs?

Arguably, we are living in an era where our thinking is more anthropocentric than it has ever been; the result of financial systems and of increased urbanisation and exploitation. We also project human emotions on to animals to an extent we have not done before, and this anthropomorphism is especially pronounced in our attitude to domesticated animals. We often regard them as members of the family, or sometimes even as our closest friends, but, while pets are therapeutic, they remain animals. I am as sentimental as anyone else over a tail-wagging Labrador with its big eyes and what I think is love, but I stop short of believing that such heart-warming behaviour is equivalent to human affection. Unlike some, I'm sure that the behaviour of pet dogs is closer to that of their wild relatives than it is to the behaviour of humans. Of course, it's not just our pets which we attempt to humanise, as naming extends to familiar animals in the wild, and even to trees, as Henry Gosse described in *The Romance of Natural History*. Further examples of our anthropomorphic approach are evident in zoos and theme parks, where we enjoy displays by orcas, sea lions or birds, thinking that the animals want to entertain us, even though we see that every move is rewarded with a tasty morsel or two. Then there is the reaction to any primate that bears its teeth and our interpretation of the behaviour as smiling or being angry.

Any newborn mammal and, especially, the 'cute' ones such as elephant calves and cheetah cubs also elicit the 'Ahh response'. I love elephant calves and can watch them for hours, often trying to work out why I do so. They are definitely honorary human beings to many and that, of course, is something which Disney capitalised on in the animated film *Dumbo*, building on an attitude that was already present in many of us. If I met an elephant calf in the wild, I am sure that my reaction would be different, especially if my presence brought an angry response from the herd. It would no doubt be the same if I came across cheetah cubs protected by their mother.

Aside from animals for which we have strong feelings of affection, we seem to be fascinated also by animals that may do us harm, or could do so if we ever co-existed. It scares us and ties in with a feeling of contact with evil. I can give several examples. On safari, people want to see the big cats, and watch them in action bringing down game. In the cinema, *Jaws* was a huge success and made devils out of great white sharks (*Carcharodon carcharias*), enhanced by numerous attacks by these fish on humans in shallow waters, many reported in grim detail on news broadcasts. Perhaps the most unusual scary animals to capture the popular imagination in this way are dinosaurs; unusual since we have no chance of seeing one alive. We manifest this fascination in films like *Jurassic Park* and in various television programmes which feature dinosaurs, supposedly brought back to life, complete with colouration and roaring sounds. I find these reconstructions rather odd and have no idea what evidence is used by programme makers as a basis for the life styles portrayed. After all, dinosaurs are only known from skeletons, or parts of bodies, but there is media interest in elaborating from the barest information, just as with stories on medicine or about life on other planets. When a new fossil dinosaur is discovered and described, it is often reported together with an artist's impression, or a computer generated presentation, of its appearance and way of life. Very few of us are interested in where this particular fossil find fits into the classification of vertebrates and we are much more interested in the awe factor. It's why dinosaurs have such a wide appeal. They are, by some margin, the most popular reptiles.

Although Henry Gosse wrote about sea serpents, and claimed them to be enaliosaurs, his interest in dinosaurs seems to end there, with the idea of relict living forms. The fossil record was always a challenge to him and, whilst recognising that geological strata and their fossilised remains of plants and animals certainly exist on Earth, this was all prochronic to him. To discuss the prochronic would be to attempt to see inside the mind of God, and Henry could not contemplate this. His interest was entirely in living forms, a contrast to that of William Pengelly. What did they talk about in their enthusiastic discussions after visiting caves and other sites in Devon? Did Henry hold to the line in *Omphalos*? We will never know.

Epilogue

Like Henry Gosse, I remain an outsider, and my Uncle Wal was perceptive in identifying that side of my character when I was young. There are the trappings of adult success – a Chair of Biology at UCL, a Doctor of Science degree, and three Teaching Prizes – but I'm still, at heart, the child who was happiest on shores, or wandering by the sea, or in the countryside. Of course, there have been many changes in my life, and one of these is perhaps unlikely; a real enjoyment of swimming. I am lucky to have a happy family life free of the tensions brought by contrasting religious beliefs, but I hope that I'm not foolish enough to think that I may never return to religion under a time of severe stress. That seems a remote possibility at present, and I think that powerful sedatives are a more likely option when the time comes. But who knows?

Concluding with an anecdote, I will always remember a comment made by one of the technicians at Durham University, Ian Dennison, as we drove out to collect research materials on the Pennine fells. I don't know what we were discussing, but Ian asked: 'Do you know your problem, Roger?' There was silence from me, before Ian provided the answer, accompanied by his wonderful, raucous laugh: 'You think too much.' Was that Henry Gosse's problem too?

---

1 *Where Adam Stood*, was broadcast on BBC 2 in 1976, and was a loose adaptation of *Father and Son*, Potter having only used a few pages as his starting point. Potter saw the play as part of a trilogy that explored individual choice in the face of seemingly omniscient forces.

2 Wotton, R, 'The Ten Plagues of Egypt', *Opticon1826*, 3. See: http://www.rogerwotton.co.uk/files/Opticon%20-%20Plagues.pdf

3 Wotton, R, 'Angels, putti, dragons and fairies: Believing the impossible', *Opticon1826*, 7. See: http://www.rogerwotton.co.uk/files/Opticon%20-%20Angels%20etc..pdf

Books published by
Philip Henry Gosse

This is not an exclusive list, but a selection of First Editions of Gosse's main titles. It is taken from Freeman and Wertheimer's *Philip Henry Gosse: A Bibliography* and this authoritative account gives a full list of Henry Gosse's publications of all types.

1840   *The Canadian Naturalist.* John Van Voorst, London. 372 pp.

1844   *An Introduction to Zoology.* Society for Promoting Christian Knowledge, London. 384 + 436 pp.

1845   *The Ocean.* Society for Promoting Christian Knowledge, London. 360 pp.

1847   *The Birds of Jamaica.* John Van Voorst, London. 448 pp. *The Monuments of Ancient Egypt, and their relation to the Word of God.* Society for Promoting Christian Knowledge, London. 358 pp.

1848   *Natural History. Mammalia.* Society for Promoting Christian Knowledge, London. 304 pp. *Illustrations of the Birds of Jamaica.* John Van Voorst, London [1848-9]. 13 parts, 52 coloured lithographs.

1849   *Natural History. Birds.* Society for Promoting Christian Knowledge, London. 327 pp. *Popular British Ornithology; containing a familiar and technical description of the birds of the British Isles.* Reeve, Benham, and Reeve, London. 320 pp.

1850   *Sacred Streams: the ancient and modern history of the rivers of the Bible.* C. Cox, London. 360 pp. *Natural History. Reptiles.* Society for Promoting Christian Knowledge, London. 296 pp.

1851   *A Text-Book of Zoology for Schools.* Society for Promoting Christian Knowledge, London. 450 pp. *A Naturalist's Sojourn in Jamaica* (assisted by Richard Hill). Longman, Brown, Green, and Longmans, London. 508 pp. *The History of the Jews, from the Christian Era to the dawn of the Reformation.* Society for Promoting Christian Knowledge, London. 400pp.

1852   *Assyria; her manners and customs, arts and arms; restored from her monuments.* Society for Promoting Christian Knowledge, London. 642 pp.

1853   *A Naturalist's Rambles on the Devonshire Coast.* John Van Voorst, London. 451 pp.

1854   *The Aquarium: an unveiling of the wonders of the deep sea.* John Van Voorst, London. 278 pp. *Natural History. Mollusca.* Society for Promoting Christian Knowledge, London. 328 pp.

1855   *A Manual of Marine Zoology for the British Isles.* John Van Voorst, London. 203 + 239 pp. [Parts I and II; Part II published in 1856].

1856   *Tenby: a sea-side holiday.* John Van Voorst, London. 400 pp.

1857   *Life in its Lower, Intermediate, and Higher Forms: or, manifestations of the divine wisdom in the natural history of animals.* James Nisbet and Co., London. 363 pp. *A Memorial of the Last Days on Earth of Emily Gosse.* James Nisbet and Co., London. 84 pp. *Omphalos: an attempt to untie the geological knot.* John Van Voorst, London. 376 pp.

1859   *Evenings at the Microscope; or researches among the minuter forms of animal life.* Society for Promoting Christian Knowledge, London. 506 pp. *Letters from Alabama, (U.S.) chiefly relating to natural history.* Morgan and Chase, London. 306 pp.

1860   *Actinologia Britannica: a history of the British sea-anemones and madrepores. With coloured figures of all the species.* John Van Voorst, London. 362 pp. [Also published in Parts from 1858-1860]. *The Romance of Natural History [First Series].* J. Nisbet and Co., London. 372 pp.

1861   *The Romance of Natural History [Second Series].* James Nisbet and Co., London. 393 pp.

1864   *Narrative Tracts* (with Emily Gosse). Morgan & Chase, London. 240 pp.

1865   *Land and Sea.* James Nisbet & Co., London. 425 pp. *A Year at the Shore.* Alexander Strahan, London. 330 pp.

1884   *The Mysteries of God: a series of expositions of Holy Scripture.* Hodder and Stoughton, London. 322pp.

1886   *The Rotifera; or wheel-animalcules* (by C. T. Hudson, assisted by P. H. Gosse). Longmans Green and Co., London. Published in two volumes. 128 + 144 pp from 6 original Parts.